Charlotte Brontë's Devotee

William Smith Williams: friend and mentor to a host of Victorian writers and artists

Philip Hamlyn Williams

Copyright © 2019 Philip Hamlyn Williams

All rights reserved.

ISBN: 9781092844062

Independently published

Cover image © The Bronte Society

DEDICATION

This book is dedicated to members of the London and South-East sub group of the Brontë Society for their advocacy and determination, and to the Society itself for its donation which, together, resulted in a new memorial of William Smith Williams being placed alongside the monument over his grave.

CONTENTS

	Acknowledgments	1
	Introduction	2
1	Childhood	5
2	Apprenticeship	17
3	Hullmandel years	37
4	House of Smith, Elder	58
5	Brontë years – Jane Eyre	71
6	Brontë years - friendship	91
7	Brontë years – art and tragedy	109
8	Brontë years – Cornhill parcels	126
9	Brontë years – a cooling	147
10	The Cornhill	165
11	Ruskin years	186
12	Legacy	211
	About the author	221
	Notes	222

ACKNOWLEDGMENTS

I thank Norman Penty for his work on William's ancestry, and the Brontë archive at Haworth, the Smith, Elder & Co. archive at the National Library of Scotland and the Ruskin archive at the University of Lancaster for all their help. I thank my new found relatives, Cheryl Pivac in New Zealand and Fran Manning and Christine Hutchison in Australia, for their family archival material. I thank Brontë biographers, but especially Rebecca Fraser for her kindness in reading my manuscript, making helpful comments and for adding her words to the cover of this volume. I thank Gemma Thomas for proof reading my draft ready for publication, although I remain responsible for any errors. I thank John Weiss & Sons, The Royal Society of Arts and Brian Speak for allowing me to use their images. I thank Amber Adams, editor of Brontë Studies, for her encouragement.

Margaret Smith's three volume edition of Charlotte Brontë's letters is a tour de force, and readers, who want to read in full Charlotte's letters to William, need look no further. However, where possible, I have referred to the originals held by the Brontë Society or to the much earlier edition by Clement Shorter. Every effort has been made to trace copyright holders of these and other letters, and to obtain their permission for the use of copyright material. I would like to apologise for any errors or omission and would be grateful to be notified of any corrections that should be incorporated in future reprints or editions of this book. My sadness is that it seems that only one of William's letters to Charlotte survives. If publication of this volume prompts revelation of others, I will gladly rewrite it. Finally, I thank Maggie, my wife of over forty years, for being so supportive as I continue to write about my family.

INTRODUCTION

William Smith Williams is known to followers of Brontë biographies as the reader for the publishers Smith, Elder & Co. who recognised the genius of Charlotte Brontë. He mentored her through her all-too-short career. But who was he? Whence had he come and whither did he go? Charles Dickens and George Meredith were also readers for other publishers, and their stories are well known, but what of William?

I was spurred on in my quest by words from a letter that his brother-in-law, Robert Hill, had written on his death: 'There were complimentary notices of his death in nearly all the papers. Nobody could have been more universally beloved or respected than he was'. I read the obituaries, and they were, indeed, full of praise and affection. In particular, one sentence in *The Publishers' Circular* caught my attention: 'The truth is that Mr Williams' previous education had fitted him to be a judge of good work, and he was singularly fair and unbiased'. I had to discover what this 'previous education' had been, but also what else he had done to merit such fulsome praise and, indeed, who those people were who loved and respected him.

I was helped in my search by the genealogical work carried out by Norman Penty and written up in his book, *The Discovery of Charlotte Brontë: William Smith Williams 1800-1875 – A Genealogical Quest*. In 2006, Penty contacted me and told me of the family tree that he had painstakingly researched. He contacted me, because my name appears in the tree as the great-grandson of William's brother, Richard. I delved into archives, books and libraries, and the wealth of material available online.

I found a true nineteenth-century Renaissance man who was as well versed in art as he was in literature, and as at home with politics as he was with science. He is known as Charlotte Brontë's mentor - a task that he carried out with devotion. However, whilst she might have been the most prominent writer, she was very far from the only one to whom William devoted his energies and very particular skills. The Brontë archive contains a magazine article by Frederick Wicks, one of the many other authors whom William encouraged, and it gives a wonderful sense of the man at his work:

> Thrusting back his massive growth of white hair, he would clasp his hands nervously in thought before delivering his opinion, and then would follow in short, pregnant sentences a perfect flood of light upon the matter in hand. He was never content with general commendation and approval, but always gave good, sound reasons and sufficient cause for all he thought. Among the many pregnant phrases that fell to my lot was one of extraordinary value as a check to the exuberance of youth. "You need," he said, "restraint – not that which checks, but that which guides the literary faculty".

I planned the biography as a quest, exploring each stage of his life. For some of those stages, particularly the Brontë years, the material is rich and plentiful; however, for others it is sketchy, and I have sought to paint a picture by drawing on the accounts of others. I uncovered articles in periodicals, a poem in praise of Keats, the paper about lithography that was delivered to the Society of Arts, and the first *Selections from the Writings of John Ruskin.* William's small office had on its walls portraits of Thackeray, Ruskin and George Eliot. He knew a great many writers and artists, and he left some remarkable progeny.

1 CHILDHOOD

We first meet William Smith Williams in the company of his parents and brother, Richard (his elder by one year), in that most imposing of buildings, St Martins-in-the-Fields. It is the occasion of his baptism and the date is 23 February 1801. Barely seven weeks earlier, the United Kingdom of Great Britain and Ireland had itself been born with William Pitt's Act of Union, sealed by King George III.[1] To what extent that would impact on a family aspiring to join the 'middling orders' must remain conjecture; the wider political picture would have profound implications.

St Martin's then was neither next to the National Gallery, nor did it overlook Trafalgar Square. The former would not be built for another quarter of a century, and the latter battle would not be fought for another four years.[2] Napoleon had not long since taken up the cudgels of the French Revolution. His army of volunteers, burning bright with the spirit of revolution, notched up swift victories whilst feasting on the lands they conquered or, as they viewed it, freed from oppression.[3] The British Army had braced itself against attack as Napoleon amassed the 'Army of England' either side of Boulogne.[4] The British economy was already suffering from the war, and a sequence of poor harvests had resulted in rocketing food prices and, thus, much hunger.

The area around St Martin's was no longer fields, but an old conglomeration of 'vile' houses, home to some of the thousands of men, women and children flocking to the capital from the countryside.[5] The process of landowners enclosing common land had been going on for centuries, but the increasing demands for food by the growing urban populations made it an imperative.[6] Revolution was afoot in the fields. The results were threefold. Food production increased. Thousands of countryfolk lost their homes and livelihoods. Landowners became ever richer.[7] The power this gave them would cloud the politics of the country into which William and his brother had been born, for most of their lives.

To view the migration to the cities, to London, as purely an escape from rural poverty would be a mistake. There were those keen to seek their fortunes in the urban bustle. There were those attracted by the availability of work. Something else, though, was going on. Men and women from disparate places and backgrounds were drawn to this crucible of creativity.

Of William's future bosses, Charles Hullmandel came from Germany, John Taylor from Edinburgh and George Smith (senior) also from Edinburgh. Germany was ruled by the same king, and Edinburgh was very much a centre of publishing. Rural Scotland, through the Highland Clearances, was undergoing the same sort of change as much of England.[8]

Of the authors whom William published, Thomas Carlyle was born in the village of Ecclefechan some hundred miles north of Edinburgh.[9] Leigh Hunt was born in London, but of parents who had returned from Philadelphia, and William Makepeace Thackeray was born in India. Even at the beginning of the nineteenth century, the tentacles of British influence reached around the globe. John Keats was also born in London, but John Clare came from Northamptonshire. John Ruskin's father, James, came from Edinburgh, Elizabeth Gaskell's father was from Berwick-upon-Tweed and, of course, Charlotte Brontë was from Haworth in Yorkshire.

Of those within his circle, George Lewes was from London, but his later partner, Mary Ann Evans (George Eliot), was from Nuneaton, Richard Horne was from Edmonton and William Hazlitt from Maidstone. Charles Wells was a Londoner.[10]

Of the painters about whom he wrote and with whom he worked, Joseph Dickinson from Northumberland and his wife from Exeter; Samuel Prout was from Plymouth and Dante Gabriel Rossetti from London.

However, all of that was for some years ahead.

William's parents, Richard and Mary, had been among those flocking to London barely a decade earlier. Norman Penty's research suggests that Richard's family came from Wheatley in Oxfordshire. Oxfordshire had suffered from landlords enclosing their land. Richard's family, though, were not farmers; their business was that of fellmongers. This ancient trade, well known in the Cotswolds, was concerned with the hides of sheep. These hides would be cured and processed for a number of uses. In the case of the Williams family, the principal use was in the making of parchment, for which a strong demand came from the neighbouring University of Oxford.

Wheatley was a village renowned for its dissident attitudes. During the Civil War, it had been a place 'in the know'; traffic travelling from Royalist Oxford to Parliamentarian London would pass through and certainly those who frequented the village inns would be well informed. It had had periodic clashes with the Bishop of Oxford. It was meant to be a village in the parish of the neighbouring and larger village of Cuddesdon, but the villagers demanded their own separate parish.[11] On the creation of the bishopric of Oxford, the bishop's residence was built at Cuddesdon - something not likely to be welcomed by dissidents. In the nineteenth century, Bishop Wilberforce, also known for his ferocious attacks on Darwin,[12] described it as 'a most difficult parish'.[13] Charlotte Brontë, in a letter, mentions a place where

William visited an old-maiden cousin and found a hamlet much run down.[14] The latter comment accords with Wilberforce's note that in the mid-nineteenth century, the villagers were suffering deprivations more often associated with overcrowded urban living.[15] I visited Wheatley and took a photograph of the house where village records show that the Williams family lived. Strip away the many houses built since the mid-nineteenth century and you are left with not much more than a hamlet. It is hilly and might, quite possibly, be taken for the Chiltern chalk mentioned in Charlotte's letter.

William's grandfather, also William, had left the village in the late eighteenth century, at which time his elder sister, Katherine, was running the family business from premises at Number 90 High Street.[16] She had inherited the house and business from her father who, it seems, had prospered. In 1775, he had advertised for two parchment-makers in *Jackson's Oxford Journal*.[17] Other family members lived close by, including Katherine's sister, 'great-aunt Susanna' a seemingly redoubtable lady whose will, Norman Penty discovered, mentions William's brother, but not William. The will of another Richard (a tallow chandler and gentleman of Banbury also a brother of Susanna) left five guineas to William's father for a ring and twenty pounds to William's aunt Rebecca, but not to his uncle Lawrence. Such are families.[18]

But, back to St Martin's. The small baptism party might have left the great church and headed east along the Strand from Charing Cross, which was the place where everyone arrived. It was the 'roaring vortex' at the heart of the London 'whirlpool'.[19] The Eleanor Cross would have been there, but not, of course, the railway station. Some sixty years would need to pass before the southern railway would thread its way over the river to its terminus just south of the cross.[20] Indeed, it would be twenty-five years before the first railway joined Stockton to Darlington. At the time of William's birth and for most of his life, the horse-drawn omnibus was the only means of mass transport in the growing metropolis.

The Strand itself was the main thoroughfare between the cities of Westminster and London. Not so many years earlier, it had been so vulnerable to attack by highwaymen that Members of Parliament, leaving Westminster to return home to London after a sitting, would travel in groups for their mutual safety. The Strand was still bordered by the remnants of medieval palaces, subsequently in-filled to provide more space for the thousands who crowded there to live. It was said that there had been lanes leading down to the river from the Strand which, in summer, would be 'resplendent with hawthorn and fragrant with honeysuckle'. At the turn of the nineteenth century, that space by the river was occupied by all sorts of 'ne'er-do-wells' and prostitutes. The river was busy with some three thousand boats and wherries for hire.[21] The Strand was equally bustling and noisy with carts and vehicles of all sizes. It was lined with smaller dwellings, many dating from Chaucer's time. There were coffee shops, taverns, eating houses and milk cellars, where cows were led underground for a fortnight before being taken back to their pastures. There were printers, publishers and booksellers - particularly second-hand bookshops south of the Strand where pornography was said to be on open sale. There were stories of writers in their cold garrets. The area was bohemian. In the streets there would be girls selling flowers and ribbons, and boys selling fruit. There was probably little you couldn't buy.

Making their way along the Strand, the baptism party would have come to Number 408,[22] just east of where the Adelphi Theatre is now, where Richard was in business with Mary Nethersole as wax and tallow chandlers.[23] Not just any wax and tallow chandler, but one by appointment to the Crown. Norman Penty searched the trade directories and found that the firm had been set up by William Nethersole in the 1770s but that he had been succeeded by his wife Mary, by 1780, who had traded under the name Mary Nethersole & Son. In 1794, Richard Williams was taken into partnership. It was, however, only his name that appeared from 1805 to 1815, although under the trading name of Nethersole & Williams.[24] All great houses had their own wax and tallow chandler, whose job it was to make candles and soap, sometimes from mutton fat. Thackeray, whom we will meet later, wrote, in *Vanity Fair*, of the boy Dobbin whose father sold mutton candles. We don't know whether the soap and candles were made on the premises or just sold from there. Equally, we don't know whether the family lived above the shop, but they quite probably did. Over two centuries later, Number 408 is just by a narrow archway through which, if you venture, you can find on your left the Nell Gwynne Tavern, which has been there since the 1600s. Venture further and you will see that you are in a narrow alley, Bull's Inn Court. It was in an area of similar narrow courts and crowded dwellings. Venture further still and you emerge into Maiden Lane just opposite Rules Restaurant. Rules was founded in 1798. Maiden Lane had been the birthplace of Turner a quarter of a century earlier. Charlotte Brontë's letters refer more than once to Turner and to William's love for his art.

A well-modelled biography would now include descriptions of William's family, their daily life and his schooling. For William, and indeed Richard, we have no such detail, but, knowing where they lived and being able to find from other accounts what life was like, we can at least gain an impression.

Their father's Royal Warrant would probably have required of him frequent visits to the residence of the monarch, George III. Would it be too farfetched to suppose that Richard might have indulged in a little understairs gossip? The king had suffered a recurrence of his mental illness in 1801, following the first bout in 1788 when his son had made his first attempt at the office of Prince Regent. 1801 was the same year that Pitt had left office after twenty or so years in government. The following dozen years would see no fewer than five occupants of Downing Street,[25] including on 11 May 1812 the assassination of Prime Minister Spencer Perceval in the Houses of Parliament. Gossip certainly would have covered the successes and setbacks of the Napoleonic Wars and the hardships that the people of this island would have had to endure, even though they had been spared invasion. It might have rejoiced in the huge spur to industrial production that the war demanded but perhaps lamented that it would change forever the face of many parts of the land.[26]

I imagine William as an inquisitive boy venturing north of Maiden Lane to stare, wide-eyed, at the fashionable bustle of Covent Garden: the vegetable market and flower girls alongside the men and women of rank attending the opera house, or perhaps the theatre in Drury Lane, as the only two theatres then licensed. As regulation loosened its grip, he would almost certainly have walked the short distance to the Lyceum and witnessed its rapidly changing programme of productions. At the end of the first decade of the nineteenth century, the Lyceum became the home, for part of the year, of the Drury Lane Company, following a fire. Fire also led it to become the home, for some years, of the renowned Beefsteak Club, whose members included royalty and notable politicians and theatrical men of the time.[27] Might William have watched the comings and goings? The Lyceum offered both theatre and opera, and its programmes from the time boasted Shakespeare, as well as lighter contemporary pieces. Some years later, William would write theatre reviews for *The Spectator, The Athenaeum* and *The Examiner*. Perhaps his love for, and fascination of, theatre was born in his childhood. But what of books? What of art? I have already mentioned the bookshops around the Strand and feel certain that a young William would have been ever-present. For art, there was Somerset House, which was home to the Royal Academy and was the largest art collection then open to public view.[28]

William's brother, Richard, would later become a surgical instrument maker and would run the London premises of Weiss & Son. These premises were also in the Strand, just to the south and west of 408. John Weiss had moved to London from Germany in 1787 and set up at Number 62 The Strand. If we can imagine William making his way along Maiden Lane to the Lyceum, then we can equally see the young Richard peering through the shop window of Number 62 and marvelling at the gleaming instruments he saw.

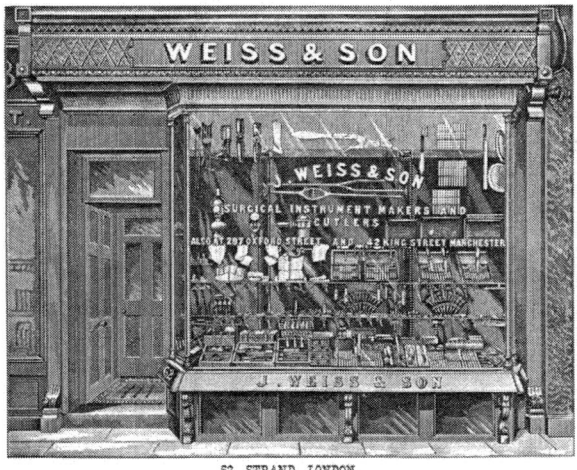

With kind permission of John Weiss & Son

Since this is a flight of fancy, then we can perhaps imagine Richard (senior) taking his elder son along to Albemarle Street, the first home of the Royal Institution, where Humphry Davy was exploring the properties of gases and, a little later, Faraday would demonstrate electricity. It would probably be wrong to think of William as the arty son and Richard as the scientist, since, later, William would write with great lucidity on the new printing process of lithography. The early nineteenth century was not a time when science and art were compartmentalised, so it may well have been the two boys with their father and mother, for that matter. This, though, is probably too much for even the imagination. Anything other than basic primary education was some decades away for most men, and certainly for women. One institution which would feature later in William's life, and which would have been of equal interest to his brother Richard, was the Society of Arts in John Adam Street between the Strand and the river. This society encouraged 'arts, manufactures and commerce'.

The boys' life in the bustle of the city was to be brought to an untimely end with the death of their mother, which we can infer from the absence of her name in her husband's will, written in November 1811. We have no notion of the cause of her death; in the London of the time cholera was never far away and was more prevalent in the crowded courts. Tragically her death was followed, soon after the execution of his will, by the death also of their father as evidenced by the proving of the will in June 1814.

Norman Penty tells that Richard's will made provision for his 'two dear sons Richard Williams and William Smith Williams', but did not appoint a guardian. The will required 'his Friends and Executors, namely John Back, Tallow Factor of Aldersgate Street City of London and Isaac Hitchin, Currier of Soho, to do all that [was] necessary to sell/dispose of his business, stock and estate to ensure that there [were] sufficient funds available to maintain the two boys and enable them to enter apprenticeships or serve in a profession or business'.[29] William's aunt and uncle were included as beneficiaries, had the boys predeceased their parents, and so it may be that their uncle or aunt acted in loco parentis. We don't know. As previously mentioned, many years later, Charlotte Brontë wrote that William had visited an old-maiden cousin,[30] probably in the family home of Wheatley. The cousin had spoken warmly of his parents, and so we may perhaps infer that extended family played a part in the boys' upbringing.

There is, however, a hint about William's continued education to be found in an anecdote of Edmund Gosse. Gosse, brother-in-law to William's son Robert, was a poet and critic born halfway through the nineteenth century and who reputedly kept a diary of the doings of his friends and acquaintances. Some of these he recorded and they are known as 'Gosse's Candid "Snapshots"'.[31] A number were compiled by academic Paul F. Mattheisen and published in a *Victorian Studies* journal in 1965. One concerns Richard

Hengist Horne. Horne was a poet born in 1802 and best known for *Orion: An Epic Poem*, published in 1843 and republished a number of times before his death in 1884. As I tell in a later chapter, Horne was also the first author to be published by the young George Smith of Smith, Elder & Co.

Gosse recorded a visit that he made to Horne on 15 February 1877 and said that Horne gave him some pieces of biography, recalling that 'he went to school at Edmonton where Charles Wells, Williams and John Keats were among his school fellows'. Mattheisen notes that Williams was probably William Smith Williams, adding that the poet, Charles Wells, later became his brother-in-law.

At first sight, this delighted me, since Keats's biographers offer a little of John Keats's school days. Keate's school, though, was in Enfield, with Keats living in nearby Edmonton, and so may have been different. Keats studied under John Clarke, whose school numbered some eighty or so boys, in a very liberal atmosphere with no beating and numerous books other than schoolbooks. It was said to have been Clarke's son, Charles Cowden Clarke, who inspired Keats greatly not least in his love of Spenser's *The Faerie Queene*. I could quite imagine this inspiration spreading to Charles Wells and also to William. Penty suggests that William might well have stayed on briefly as a teacher after leaving Clarke's school. He also wonders whether William's future father-in-law, Francis Hill, who was a teacher in nearby Broxbourne, might have had some sort of teaching contact with the boys. He points out that one of the Hill's children was named Anna Maria Wells Hill, perhaps indicating a family connection with Wells.[32]

William also appears at some length in a reminiscence by another late Victorian writer, Theodore Watts-Dunton, of Wells's relationship with Dante Gabriel Rossetti who championed Wells's epic poem *Joseph and His Brethren*.[33] This poem will reappear from time to time in William's story. For now, though, I have to note that, whilst the reminiscence talks much of William and Wells, and of Wells's, Horne's and Keats's schooldays, it makes no reference to William being part of them.

Perhaps we are none the wiser as to William's schooling. This, in the context of a quest to discover William's education, is something of a drawback. It is not a fatal one as will become clear as I explore the next stage in his life as an apprentice to publishers Taylor & Hessey.

2 APPRENTICESHIP

'William Smith Williams began his active life in 1817 as an apprentice to the publishing firm of Taylor & Hessey': so reads the entry in the *Dictionary of National Biography*, an imprint of Smith, Elder & Co. I looked behind these rather anodyne words and found a world buffeted from all sides by revolution. The eighteenth century had been a time of discovery, largely by people, such as Joseph Banks, from privileged backgrounds; the nineteenth was going to see repeated attempts by ordinary men and women to throw open the doors of privilege for all. Arguments about the extension of the suffrage were to be found everywhere; the French Revolution had indeed let that genie out of the bottle.

Printing had been invented some three centuries earlier and had caused its own revolution, not least in opening up the Bible to those other than clergy who walked a life of faith. However, books were the preserve of the wealthy. They were objects of beauty to be treasured as any great art, and so not available to the common man or woman. Literacy was the preserve of the few. The publishing world, at the time of William's childhood and for a while after, was dominated by a few highly respected firms producing fine volumes of great beauty – and price. Aileen Fyfe suggests that, in the 1820s, a copy of Walter Scott's novel *Kenilworth* would have cost 31s 6d.[34] She puts this into context by quoting weekly wages for lower-ranking professionals at 40s. Even for a skilled compositor, buying a new book would be beyond their dreams. There were reasons for this high cost.

Paper was still made by hand. There were hundreds of paper mills around the country, but their processes were both slow and laborious. Pulped linen and cotton rags would be poured onto a wire mesh, where it would be pressed onto felt and then left to dry for as long as a month. The prodigious growth in cotton production, as a result of industrialisation, meant that shortages of earlier periods were a thing of the past by 1830.[35] Nevertheless, it was an expensive and laborious process. Print was still composed by hand, with letters being set in a frame, ink applied, and the whole thing being pressed carefully onto a paper sheet. The process would be repeated on the reverse side of the paper. The sheets would then be folded, cut and stitched before being bound. The cost of printing was, thus, significant. It was a highly skilled trade and one where the skilled compositors were well paid, even if their weekly wage of 25s. couldn't stretch to the price of a single novel. Also in relation to cost, the French Revolution comes to be quoted once more, since, even after the defeat of Napoleon, the government was fearful of too much news and comment reaching too many people; accordingly, taxes were levied on paper, advertising and publication. The tax on paper was 3d. per pound weight and a stamp of 4d. was required on each newspaper. The tax on advertisements put them beyond the reach of most businesses. It was only in time that the taxes reduced, but they would not disappear until the 1860s.

Things, though, were to change. In the latter part of the eighteenth century, the descendants of those same people who had had the Bible revealed to them through printing began to see it as their duty to open up books (principally the Bible itself but also improving religious tracts) to the masses. The Sunday School movement and the Evangelical churches were encouraging reading by many more people and, once able to read, these people formed a market for the printed word.[36] Their demand was, in part, satisfied by re-prints of the classics for which copyright no longer applied, but also by tracts and pamphlets. Cheap 'hack' writing came out of Grub Street, and the first of the 'penny dreadfuls' began to appear, building on the popularity of the Gothic novels of the late eighteenth century. More and more people were able to read and so hungered for any printed material they could lay their hands on.

The publishing world responded in a number of related ways. The mechanisation of the production of paper came, to a large degree, as a result of the efforts of one man: John Dickinson.[37] Dickinson embraced the science of paper-making and perfected a cartridge paper suitable for use with artillery. The concept of a commercial paper-making machine had been conceived in 1803 by Henry and Sealy Fourdrinier, using a continuous wire mesh on which the pulp was poured. In her book, *Steam-Powered Knowledge*, Aileen Fyfe suggests that these two had given insufficient attention to securing their patents which meant that others could take and then develop their ideas.[38] The *John Dickinson* history suggests that these early machines also had drawbacks only overcome by later techniques such as those patented by Dickinson himself in 1811.[39] Essentially the Dickinson process involved a wire mesh cylinder immersed in liquid pulp. A reliable supply of clean water was vital, and Dickinson found his at Apsley Mill near Hemel Hempstead in Hertfordshire. It is, perhaps, not too fanciful to suggest that William learnt of these new processes whilst in neighbouring Broxbourne. The parallel invention of steam-driven printing presses by Koenig in 1810, using a cylindrical platen to roll paper over the flat typeset, enabled faster printing particularly suitable for newspapers.[40] Other developments added significantly to the ability of publishers to reduce the cost of the printed word, making it available to the wider reading public. Original type was considered too valuable to be kept made up, and stereotyping allowed typeset to be copied, and so reused. Other forms of reproducing images, (not least lithography as I discuss in Chapter 3) enabled their inclusion in cheaper publications.

Fyfe offers some statistics. The highest circulation newspaper in 1851, the year of the Great Exhibition, was *The Times* with thirty-eight thousand copies sold daily. This compared with a circulation of only eleven thousand bi-weekly in 1830. As for books, Fyfe suggests a figure of two thousand new titles in 1800 to four thousand in 1840.[41]

That, then, was the world which William entered in 1817, except that many of the smaller publishers, including Taylor & Hessey would, to their cost, steer around technical advances and continue with the old methods of production certainly for small runs as was the case with many of their titles.

So, what of Taylor & Hessey? Edmund Blunden, who had written a biography of Keats, published a biography of John Taylor,[42] partner in Taylor & Hessey, which sheds light on the life that William probably led. He tells how John Taylor, originally from Edinburgh, and James Augustus Hessey entered into partnership in 1806. They had met whilst apprenticed to East Retford publisher Vernor & Hood. Taylor was the literary man and Hessey, with 'gentlemanly connections', the bookseller. On moving to London, they lived and worked at 93 Fleet Street, close to St Bride's church. They shared the house with three other bachelors: Frederick Falkner (who would become Hessey's brother in law), F.W. Haden and George Stothert. As publishers and booksellers, how they set out their stall becomes clear in an advertisement from 1810:

> A very extensive and choice selection of Elegant Books, comprising the best editions of the the works of every author of merit in Polite and

> General English Literature, bound in the most beautiful and splendid manner in calf, Russian leather, Morocco, vellum &c, &c. and many of them ornamented and illustrated with original drawings, the whole peculiarly adapted for presents of a superior description, is now on sale at Taylor & Hessey's, 93 Fleet St, where a catalogue has been published and may be had gratis.[43]

Blunden added that he had seen in modern catalogues that Taylor & Hessey 'made a thing of fore-edge painting'. Most certainly Taylor & Hessey viewed their books as things of beauty.

In 1812 a third and essential member of Taylor & Hessey joined in the person of lawyer Richard Woodhouse, a school friend from Bath of the others who lived at Number 93. Taylor wrote to his father about both Hessey and Woodhouse, and, of the latter, said, 'he joins us in our Essay writing and debates – in which he engages solely as we do for improvement'.[44] The group he joined was known as the Philological Society, which had first met on 8 January 1812 at the Queen's Arms Tavern. Improvement was key; Taylor himself studied Classics. This, then, was the environment which William entered as he embarked on his career. In an age when only very few attended university, this kind of self-help group was the way in which bright young men would make their way in the world. The mention of a Philological Society prompted me to explore further. There still exist a number of societies by that name whose purpose is the scholarly study of language and languages. The London Society, which claims to be the oldest, traces its origins back to 1830 and was a society founded within the University of London.[45] That Taylor and friends were functioning in a society outside a university some years before then goes further to underline the status of self help in nineteenth century education.

The partners endeavoured to be commercially successful, and Blunden writes that among their best selling titles were two by a Mrs Taylor of Ongar including *Practical Hints for Young Females, on the Duties of a Wife, a Mother, and a Mistress of a Family*. This surely has more than an echo of rising levels of literacy among, in this case, young women who were aspiring to join the growing numbers of people who were no longer working class, but for whom the gentility of aristocracy was a dream beyond reach.

By 1816, it seems that the business was strong enough to venture into the world that was Taylor's passion: poetry, for in that year Taylor& Hessey's list included the second edition of Leigh Hunt's *The Story of Rimini*. [46] Leigh Hunt was, at that time, both celebrated and notorious. He was a Romantic poet descended from families from Ireland and Barbados. He was, for years, 'a scourge of the corrupt regency establishment, a dauntless moderniser who called for parliamentary reform, freedom of the press, sexual equality and liberty of conscious'. Nicholas Roe, writing his in book *Fiery Heart: The First Life of Leigh Hunt,* is at pains to move away from views of Hunt from his later life where 'he survives as the original of Charles Dickens's feckless Harold Skimpole in *Bleak House*'. Hunt had, with his brother, founded the radical periodical *The Examiner,* for which William would later become a contributor of reviews. In its section '*The Political Examiner*', Hunt would offer his critique of current politics. King George III's final illness of 1810 had resulted in his son's appointment as Prince Regent and Hunt wrote repeatedly of the shortcomings of the Regency. *The Examiner* successfully defended a number of libel cases, but on 9 December 1812, Hunt stood in the dock, with his brother, charged with 'intention to traduce and vilify his Royal Highness the Prince of Wales, Regent of the United Kingdom, and to bring his Royal Highness into hatred, contempt and disgrace'. They appeared before Lord Ellenborough, who had sentenced the elderly Daniel Eaton to eighteen months and one hour standing in the pillory for publishing Thomas Paine's *The Age of Reason*.[47] Two months later, and to his great shock, Hunt was sent to Surrey Gaol for two years.

On leaving prison, Hunt got to know Charles Cowden Clarke and, through him, John Keats who was much inspired by *The Story of Rimini*. The name of Hunt will appear time and again in William's story. A number of writers who mention William certainly suggest that the two knew each other in the 1820s. It appears that Hunt and Taylor fell out over money, and Hunt found an alternative publisher elsewhere. In the 1830s Hunt would be published by Moxon, the celebrated publisher of Tennyson.[48]

So, combined with the atmosphere of self improvement, William encountered the sharply radical. This might well have gelled for him with the 'family myth', that we are descended from Oliver Cromwell. In her book *Cromwell – Our Chief of Men*, Antonia Fraser tells how, in the fifteen hundreds, Cromwell's great-grandfather, Richard who had been born Williams, adopted the surname of his rather more famous uncle Thomas.[49] I have been unable to trace a link back to that Richard Williams.

In 1817, Taylor & Hessey took over from the Ollier brothers as Keats's publishers. Blunden tells how Ollier had written to Keats on 29 April 1817 to sever their connection with the young poet. Taylor welcomed him with (nearly) open arms. Keats, like Hunt, was one of the 'cockney' poets; Taylor's tastes were then more traditional. Keats's first work to be published by Taylor was his poem *Endymion*, which Taylor published in quarto, thought of then as rather traditional. We can perhaps imagine William and his colleagues, among the whole of the small staff at Taylor & Hessey, waiting on the verdict of the critics - in particular the influential *Quarterly Review*, which John Murray, one of the larger publishers, had set up in 1809 as a competitor to the longer-established *Edinburgh Review*. It was fiercely Tory establishment, defending both Church and Crown. Sir Walter Scott was a great supporter. With this background, it could hardly have surprised anyone that its view on *Endymion* was 'malevolent', and *Blackwoods* Magazine, described by Blunden as the 'red-nosed comedian of Regency culture', was no better.[50] Keats continued to write, despite the sometimes cruel criticism. 1819 saw the publication of *La Belle Dame sans Merci* the first verse of which surely brings memories of schooldays:

> O what can ail thee, knight-at-arms,
> Alone and palely loitering?
> The sedge has withered from the lake,
> And no birds sing.

The *Ode to a Nightingale* also appeared in print for the first time. William was utterly enthralled.

William's friend Charles Wells met Keats, and they became close friends. Wells would also never be very far away from William's path. Watts-Dunton, in his *Reminiscence of Kelmscott Manor*, offers a vivid picture of Wells when he calls him a vagabond. Wells, with Keats's brother Tom and R.H. Horne, was part of Keats's set. Watts-Dunton suggests that Keats's own 'animal spirits were of the exuberant kind'. Those who knew Wells in his youth described him, with his sparkling blue eyes, red curls, and bluff, rather blowsy complexion, as a 'bright, quick, most piquant lad, overflowing with wit and humour'.[51] Norman Penty has this to say about Keats and Wells:

> Charles Jeremiah Wells, William's future brother-in-law and possible school friend, was also very friendly with all the Keats boys and in June/July 1816 received a sonnet from John Keats in return for a present of roses he had sent to him. From the tone of the sonnet it is clear that the two men were on extremely friendly terms and we know,

from Keats's letters, that during the period 1816 to 1818 they regularly dined together, held drinking sessions, went to the theatre, attended poetry lectures and that Keats stayed with Wells at his parents' home in Featherstone Buildings, Holborn on several occasions.[52]

He goes on to observe that there is no mention of William, but that he would be surprised if he had not been part of the circle. In addition, William was influenced by William Hazlitt who, in 1818, also joined Taylor's list with *Lectures on the English Poets*. Hazlitt, son of a Methodist minister, had first set out to become a minister himself. He then tried painting, but finally settled on writing about liberal politics – he was a firm supporter of the French Revolution – and later on literary and theatrical criticism. Hazlitt and Wells also became friends. A circle of literary friendships was beginning which would last the whole of William's life. It would be remiss also not to remind readers that Kelmscott Manor, which Watts-Dunton was remembering, was the home of William Morris, a friend of members of the Pre-Raphaelite Brotherhood and of John Ruskin: further names which will reappear in William's story.

It was said that by 1819, Taylor & Hessey had achieved 'respectability', notwithstanding their bias towards reforming writers, and it was to this environment that the young William Smith Williams committed his working hours. I suspect also that Fleet Street was an exciting place to work. In August 1819 reports would have filtered down from Manchester of the Peterloo Massacre. Katharine Viner of *The Guardian* tells how a young reporter, John Edward Taylor, attended a peaceful rally of some sixty thousand people addressed by the radical Henry Hunt. William Hazlitt had written a year earlier that 'nothing that was established was to be tolerated … the world was to be turned topsy-turvy'.[53] The authorities were so concerned by the mob that they ordered their troops to attack and many were killed or injured. Taylor witnessed what happened but also saw that *The Times* correspondent had been arrested and he was concerned that the story might never reach London. 'So Taylor rushed a report on to the night coach to London, got it into *The Times*, and thus turned a Manchester demonstration into a national scandal'. Taylor went on to found *The Manchester Guardian* two years later. The issue that concerned the Manchester protestors was once again that of the suffrage. Jane Robinson tells how a great many groups of both men and women were agitating to be given the vote.[54] The establishment was adamant that it would not budge. This is an issue that will reappear more than once in William's story.

In 1819, also, the poet John Clare came to Taylor & Hessey, through contact made by Taylor's cousin Edward Drury. Quickly, Clare's work began to represent a high proportion of their annual publications, and John Taylor himself invested much time and guidance into Clare's career. In 1820 Taylor published his *Poems Descriptive of Rural Life and Scenery* and the following year *The Village Minstrel*. Charles Lamb, a friend of Hazlitt who was much loved for his *Tales from Shakespeare*, also joined the list that year. Yet, in spite of these impressive names, an analysis of the Taylor & Hessey's business suggests that none of the literary works were, in fact, profitable and that a good proportion of the annual list were religious tracts. The article suggests that many commentators had previously seen Taylor & Hessey as bring on a par with Longman or Murray, whereas it was much smaller but seeming to punch well above its weight.[55] For William, and for others working there, this was undoubtedly of huge benefit, giving them exposure to some of the leading literary names of the day.

By 1820, Keats's health was deteriorating and funds were collected for him to go to a more suitable climate in Rome. 17 September 1820 was a day that William had perhaps dreamed of for some years and quite possibly remembered for the rest of his life. On that day John Keats embarked on what was to be his final voyage to Rome. Blunden tells how, at Tower Dock, Taylor, Keats's friend Haslam and Woodhouse went on board the ship, the *Maria Crowther*, on which Keats was to sail. William had accompanied Keats in his carriage to the docks, for 'any last minute errands'. This unremarkable event is recorded by a number of Brontë biographers, with the implication that William had been chosen because he already knew Keats. Blunden points to a rather remarkable piece of writing, which was probably William's first published work and which appeared in *Hone's Table Book* as a eulogy to Keats, following his untimely death in 1821. The words are attributed to 'Gaston' whom Blunden recognises as none other than William. In Hone's edition there is first a short letter and then a poem. This is how it appears:

Memorials of John Keats
To the Editor,

The anecdote of Keats, which appeared in the late number of your *Table Book* recalled his image to my "mind's eye" as vividly, through the tear of regret, as the long buried pictures on the walls of Pompeii appear when water is thrown over them; and I turned to re-peruse the written record of my feelings, at hearing him spoken of a few months since. These lines I trouble you with, thinking that they may gratify the feelings of some one of his friends, trusting their homeliness maybe pardoned for the sake of the feeling which dictated them.

I should also be glad of this opportunity to express the wishes of many of his admirers for a portrait of Keats. There are two in existence; one, a spirited profile sketch by Haydon; the other a beautiful miniature by his friend Severn; but neither had been engraved. Mr Severn's return to England will probably produce some memorial of his "span of life" and a more satisfactory account of his last moments than can be gleaned from report. The opportunity that would thus be afforded of giving to the world the posthumous remains of his genius, will, it is to be hoped, not be neglected. Such a volume would be incomplete without a portrait; which, if seen by the most prejudiced of his literary opponents, would turn the laugh of contempt into a look of thoughtful regret. Hoping my rhymes will not frustrate my wishes, I remain, Sir,

   Your obliged correspondent,
   and humble servant,
   Gaston
   Sept. 13, 1827.

Thy name dear Keats is not forgotten quite
E'en in this dreary pause – Fame's dark twilight –
This space betwixt death's starry-vaulted sky,
And the bright dawn of immortality.
That time where tear and elegy lie cold
Upon the barren tomb, and ere enrolled
Thy name up on the list of honour men,
In the world's volume writ with History's lasting pen.

No! there are some who in their bosom's haven
Cherish thy mem'ry - on whose hearts are graven
The living recollections of thy worth
Thy frank sincerity, thine ardent mirth;
That nobleness of spirit, so allied
To those high qualities it quick descried
In others' natures, that by sympathy
It knit with them in friendship's strongest hold
Th' enthusiasm which thy soul pervaded
The deep poetic feeling, which invaded
The narrow channel of thy streams of life,
And wrought therein consuming, inward life.
Do those who knew thee dwell upon, and have
Derived a cordial fresh remembrance
Of thee, as though there are wert but in a trance.

CHARLOTTE BRONTË'S DEVOTEE

I, too, can think of thee with friendship's glow,
Who but at a distance only did thee know;
And oft thy gentle form flits past my sight
In transient daydreams, and a tranquil light,
Like that of warm Italian skies, comes o'er
My sorrowing heart – I feel thou art no more –
Those mild pure skies thou long'st to look upon,
Till friends, in kindness, bade thee oft 'Begone
To that more genial clime, and breathe the air
Of southern shores; thy wasted strength repair.'
Then all the Patriot burst upon thy soul;
Thy love of country made thee shun the goal
(as thou prophetically felt 't would be)
of this last pilgrimage. Though cross'd the sea,
Leaving thy heart and hopes in England here,
And went as doth a corpse upon its bier!

Still do I see thee on the river's strand
Take thy last step upon thy native land –
Still feel the last kind pressure of thy hand.
A calm dejection in thy youthful face,
To which e'en sickness lent a tender grace –
A hectic bloom – the sacrificial flower
Which marks th' approach of Death's all-withering power.

Oft do my thoughts keep vigil at thy tomb
Across the sea, beneath the walls of Rome;
And even now a tear will find its way,
Heralding pensive thoughts which thither stray.
How they must mourn who feel what I but have!
What can assuage their poignancy of woe
If I, a stranger, (save that I had been
Where thou wast, and thy gentleness has seen)
Now feel mild sorrow and a welcome sadness
As then I felt, whene'erI saw thee, gladness.
Mine was a friendship all upon one side;

Thou knewest me by name and nought beside.
In my humble station, I but shar'd the smile
Of which some trivial thought might thee beguile!
Happy in that – proud but to hear thy voice
Accost me: inwardly did I rejoice
To gain a word from thee, and if a thought
Stray'd into utterance, quick the words I caught.
I laid in wait to catch a glimpse of thee,
And plann'd where'er thou wert that I might be.
I look'd on thee as a superior being,
Whom I felt sweet content in merely seeing:
With thy fine qualities I stor'd my mind,
And now thou'rt gone, their mem'ry stays behind.
Mixt admiration fills my heart, not can
I tell which most to love – the Poet or the Man.
November 1826[56]

Three family events, which begin to add flesh to this man who, so far has only really been imagined, are recorded in William's life between Keats's death from tuberculosis on 23 February 1821 and the publication of this poem.

On 21 December 1824, William and his friend Charles Wells both attended the wedding of James Drew and Hannah Maria Powell - a relative of the two sisters whom William and Wells would marry. Some six months later William alone was recorded as being present at Wells's marriage to Emily Jane Hill at St Mary's, Whitechapel on 15 July 1825. It seems that family relationships might have been a little strained because, Penty suggests, Emily was only eighteen at the time. William, nonetheless, stood by his friend.[57]

William married Margaret Eliza Hill on 14 January 1826 at Broxbourne where a full Hill contingent was shown as present. Charles Wells, of course, was there with his new wife Emily, but there was also Charles Deacon.

A further word first about Margaret's parents and the Deacon family. Margaret's father, Francis Hill was indeed a teacher and the 1841 census return suggests that he was a headmaster. This is confirmed also by a High Court case in which he was mentioned. The census return for the Broxbourne Free School includes the names of the boy boarders and among them were Albert Deacon (aged eight) and Richard Deacon (aged ten), older brothers of Frank Deacon, whom, we shall see later, became the second husband of the widow of William's eldest son. Their parents though were James and Sophia, and not Charles.[58] The name Deacon will reappear on a number of occasions in William's story. Some years later, in William's youngest daughter's obituary, Harry Collings Deacon is mentioned as a musician friend of William who was involved in her musical education. Harry C Deacon was brother to Letitia who, we will see, acted as governess in the Williams household; her name was included in their 1861 census return. The role of governess will indeed be another recurring theme in William's story.

Two other names appear at William's wedding: Ann Williams and Thomas Fleetwood. There is an Ann Williams in William's family tree, but, by then, she would have been quite old. One name is perhaps conspicuous by its absence: William's brother Richard Williams. It might have been that the two brothers were brought up separately following their parent's death or might otherwise have grown apart. There is some suggestion that their paths might have crossed later in their lives. As Richard's great-grandson, I know that my father spoke of William and members of his family; indeed he recalled meeting William's son Richard shortly after the First World War and there is a suggestion that Richard's wife, Marian, taught music to my father's first wife. So, it might be that any growing apart was not permanent. It may though not have been a growing apart at all. We always thought that William's brother, my great-grandfather, had two children, my grandfather, Alfred and his sister Mary. However, I found in the record of Alfred's baptism, in

1831, the baptism also of William Fleetwood Williams born in 1826. It might have been that Richard and his wife were too occupied with their new child to attend the wedding. It might also explain Thomas Fleetwood's presence at the wedding as a family friend.

William, it seems, was embraced by the Hill family. Francis Hill and his wife, Margaret (née Powell), had a large family. Apart from Margaret and Emily, a third daughter Anna Maria Wells Hill was born on 11 December, 1809. Their first son, Francis Hill Jnr, followed on 30 October 1811. Charles Hill was born in June 1814 and Robert Hill on 9 July 1816. By the time Sophia Louisa Hill was born on 2 July 1819, she had three sisters and three brothers. Sophia would emigrate to Australia and good fortune has resulted in the preservation of a number of letters written to her by other members of the family.[59] I have drawn on these at relevant points in the story; they were obviously a close family - something that must have given William some compensation for losing his own parents so early in his life. What wasn't compensation was the death of Margaret Powell barely six months after William and Margaret's wedding.

For William, apart from marriage, much of the focus of this period revolved around Charles Wells and the village of Broxbourne. William, although occupied as an apprentice in Fleet Street did, according to Watts-Dunton, enjoy fishing with Wells in Broxbourne (I assume on the River Lea well known for its fine Barbel). They also founded The Phoenix Boat Club for literary men. Watts-Dunton gleaned his information from conversations with the then elderly William, and so it is entirely possible that memories became blurred, for Watts-Dunton suggests that Wells met William through Emily. Either way, as becomes clear from Charlotte Brontë's letters to William, Broxbourne and the Hill family would play an important role in his life.

In the 1820s Wells was working on his epic poem,

CHARLOTTE BRONTË'S DEVOTEE

Joseph and His Brethren. Watts-Dunton describes how he showed it to Hazlitt who told him, 'I have read your poem. I consider it shows great genius; and I advise you to stick to your profession'. The advice, it seems, was rather two-sided since Wells's then profession was law; he was practising as a solicitor. Watts-Dunton expresses a disdain for Hazlitt and a strong dislike of the advice he gave. He then presents Horne's very positive view of the poem and his encouragement for Wells to follow a career of poetry. The poem is long, and it is perhaps invidious to quote passages from it. Nonetheless the poem was destined to surface periodically during William's life, and so is important. It is divided into acts and this is the first part of the prologue:

> In the dim age when yet the rind of earth,
> Unworn by time, gave eager nature life,
> Zealous to furnish what the seasons wore
> That in a vigorous brightness flourished;
> When light and dark and constellations bright,
> The splendid sun, the silent gliding moon,
> Govern'd men's
> Habits; taught them when to thrive,
> To rest, and sleep; till, full of temperate years,
> Rude in their art, and ignorant of all
> Save passions and affections wild, untaught,
> They sank like giants in an earthy pit,
> Leaving the generation of their days
> "Twixt grief and reverence to mourn their loss
> And miss them from village and the field;
> God's voice (that mingled up the beauteous world,
> Inlaid pure heaven, and sweetly colour'd it;
> And with the wondrous magic of the clouds
> Enveils the sacred flooring evermore,
> Without bright golden, but within more rare)
> Was then upon the earth and with men's ears
> Creating reverence and faith and love.

Jacob was gone into the vale of years....

The poem was published in 1824. Watts-Dunton writes about it in a way that will surprise the modern reader, since the poem is largely forgotten. It is of course the biblical story of Joseph, but Wells writes it in Shakespearean form. This is some of what Watts-Dunton wrote:

> 'There was a time when *Joseph and his Brethren'*, says Mr Gosse in the Encyclopaedia Britannica, 'became a kind of Shibboleth – a rite of initiation into the true poetic culture'. No young poet at one time dare show his face at 16 Cheyne Walk [home to Dante Gabriel Rossetti] or at Madox Brown's great studio in Fitzroy Square[....]who could not utter the Shibboleth. The so-called Pre-Raphaelite poets[...]including Edmund Gosse himself had to read *Joseph and his Brethren* in order to exist. Carefully and anxiously was the copy at the British Museum thumbed by many an aspirant to poetic fame.[60]

Notwithstanding this, Wells, finding his poem languishing in the public eye, headed abroad. The presence of the names Dante Gabriel Rossetti, Maddox Brown and Edmund Gosse is significant in painting the picture of the circle in which William would live.

William was still employed by Taylor & Hessey, and, in 1821, they embarked on the publication of *The London Magazine*. This magazine had been founded in 1732 and continues to be published to the present day.[61] In its lifetime, it has been owned by a variety of people. Under Taylor & Hessey it became a success featuring Essays by Hazlitt and others, Poems, including those of Keats and Clare, and Reviews, as well as a regular Agricultural Report and Commercial Report. Blunden writes of the contributors to The London having a great 'team spirit': they referred to themselves as the Mary-le-Bone Eleven. In September 1821, The London Magazine published the first part of Thomas De Quincey's *Confessions of an English Opium-Eater, Being an Extract from the Life of a Scholar*. This work shocked the reading public with its vivid description of the lives of the poor, but more so with its equally vivid portrayal of addiction. De Quincey recalled Taylor with admiration but noted in him a strong religious dissent. In this context, Taylor published Samuel Taylor Coleridge's *Aids to Reflection,* in which he bypassed the theology of the day and looked back to scripture itself and the writing of the early divines. It became a spiritual handbook widely used in both Britain and the USA and in a number of editions. William was thus coming into contact with religious dissent and those parts of life that quite probably the Hills would know little of.

William would enjoy a lifelong friendship with one of the final authors to join Taylor's list: Thomas Carlyle with his *Life of Friedrich Schiller.* It might well have been that, since Taylor and Hessey were much occupied with worries about the business, their now senior apprentice, William, was given some responsibility for Carlyle's book and thereby got to know him. In later years William's daughter recalled that Carlyle was a regular visitor at the Williams house. Carlyle, along with Ruskin, who will also feature significantly in William's story, were two of the great thinkers of the 19th century. Of Carlyle, Alan Shelston writes:

> For his own generation Carlyle was not simply a contributor to the Victorian social and intellectual debate, and not simply a particularly dramatic historian, he was a prophetic voice crying out with clarity and conviction amidst the apparent confusion of an age of change.[62]

Carlyle's passion for making books widely available is evidenced in his founding of the London Library in 1841.

So, in the mid-1820s, William had declared through poetry, at the very least, an admiration for Keats. He had enjoyed literary friendship with Wells, Hazlitt, Carlyle and others. He had married and been embraced by his wife's family. He had worked in a firm of publishers which brought him close to the work of some of the great poets and thinkers of the age, to religious dissent, to radical politics and to an atmosphere steeped in self-improvement. More immediately, he had lost his job. The state of the book trade, and the approach that Taylor & Hessey adopted to it, resulted in 'disastrous' finances and the dissolution of their partnership. Taylor kept his copyrights and these would continue to benefit him and his estate for decades to come. Keats might not have sold well in his lifetime, but later he did indeed sell very well.

William decided to open a bookshop. The place he chose was Sweetings Alley at the back entrance to where the Royal Exchange buildings are now, in the City of London. Penty discovered from the 1828/30 Pigot's Directory of London that it was probably a single storey lock-up shop.[63] The City of London then was a place where Londoners both lived and worked. William and Margaret lived across the road in Poultry, in rented rooms above some trade premises. On 15 October 1826, their first child, Ellen, was born there. The Williams family returned to Margaret's home church at Broxbourne for Ellen's baptism on 14 January 1827 - the first anniversary of their wedding.

I try to picture William's shop. Dark, cold in winter, smelly from the pervading stench of London, particularly, in the summer. My suspicion is that the books would be mainly second-hand, given the high cost of new books. There would be some new and, again, I suspect, poetry would feature frequently. There would be novels: Scott was then becoming increasingly popular with *The Heart of Midlothian* and *Peveril of the Peak*. Jane Austen's *Pride and Prejudice* had been published in 1813 followed by *Persuasion*, posthumously, in 1818. Mary Shelley's *Frankenstein* had been published in in 1818[64]. There might have been works around the political and social issues of the age, such as Mary Wollstonecraft's *A Vindication of the Rights of Woman*. William sold stationery and I would have expected illustrated books with fine engravings of paintings, perhaps. I say fine engravings of paintings since, when the shop failed after some two years, William took employment with Charles Hullmandel, the pioneer of lithography (a revolutionary method of reproducing images on paper for comparatively cheap and wide distribution). William's own interest in the reproduction of images was perhaps already evident from his letter about Keats.

3 HULLMANDEL YEARS

George Smith tells, in his autobiography, how he found William languishing as a not-very-good bookkeeper at the lithographers Charles Hullmandel & Co. William had worked there for the seventeen years following the closure of his bookshop, and I couldn't accept that this was the whole story. I embarked on a quest to find out more.

Charles Hullmandel was both pioneer and evangelist for his groundbreaking technology, lithography. This process, whereby a drawing made upon a particular type of stone may be transferred by a printing press onto paper, had been in its infancy during William's childhood and teenage years. The process was discovered by Aloys Senefelder in Munich in 1800. I say discovered, since it is based upon chemistry. Calcareous stones can receive both grease and water. If a drawing is made on the stone with a greasy pen or chalk, and the stone is then wetted with water, any greasy ink then applied will adhere to the greasy line, but will be repelled by the water. Paper pressed against the stone will then take a reverse facsimile of the drawing. The art of lithography was practised with success in Germany, and, in 1817, it was taken up in Paris where it was learnt by Hullmandel. He then moved to London, taking premises at 51 Great Marlborough Street.

He was met with much suspicion from traditionalists, who believed that engraving into metal or wood was the only true way of reproducing images. John Ruskin used a particular engraver for his illustrations right to the end of his career. For others, lithography offered much that they had long sought. The artists themselves could draw on the stone, albeit in mirror image. The stone would faithfully reproduce the image many times over and at a cost far lower than engraving, meaning that illustration became available to many more people. It became a mass market.

Hullmandel wrote two papers to counter the arguments, to provide practical advice to would-be practitioners and to promote his new process. The first was his translation in 1819 from a French paper written by the pioneering lithographer M Brégeaut, which focussed on printing from the stone.[65] The second was his own, *The Art of Drawing on Stone,* 'giving a full explanation of the various styles, of the different methods to be employed to ensure success and the Modes of Correcting as well as the several Causes of failure'. This was published in 1824. It seems, from reading Hullmandel's paper, that as much opposition was derived from inexpert use of lithography as from those who wished to preserve traditional methods. It is also clear that the artist needed both talent in drawing and skill in working with stone. Probably of equal importance was the make-up of the greasy pen and chalk, the paper and the ink. Interestingly, possibly for William, a good part of the grease was derived from tallow.

William, thus, had joined a forward-looking company using the latest technology to make art available to many more than the few who could afford engravings. This was happening when the printing press had become mechanised and when paper was no longer made by hand. Revolutionary times.

William's young family took the opportunity afforded by the loss of the bookshop to move away from the crowded city to Paddington. London was growing rapidly, and the village of Paddington had, by the mid eighteenth century, been joined to that of Islington in the east by the 'New Road' (now Marylebone, Euston and Pentonville Roads). This road marked the northernmost reaches of the expanding city. To the south of it, Bloomsbury had been developed on the Bedford Estate and Mayfair on the Grosvenor Estate. This was a modern city, with many of the dwellings being less than fifty years old. It was, though, a city divided. If we take the curve of the current Regent Street, to the east 'the poor' lived in old, unhealthy and crowded housing; to the west were spacious streets and fine town houses, home to the wealthy.

Paddington itself would benefit from the building boom of the 1820s, with the plan for what was first known as Tyburnia published in 1827; unfortunately for William, work did not begin for another ten years. Elsewhere in Paddington was what was known as Tomlin's New Town, a 'shanty town of wooden hovels'[66] built on church lands. Paddington Green was an existing village with, presumably, existing village housing. We don't know exactly where William and Margaret lived, but we do know that, in that house, they added to their small family; Fanny Emily was born on 24 January 1829, William Francis on 13 January 1831 and Mary Louisa in 1832. Penty found a record of Mary's baptism at Bayswater[67]. The first three of William's children had been baptised in the church in Broxbourne where he had married Margaret. His father-in-law, Francis, was church clerk as well as headmaster, so a strong family link would have drawn them there. The village scene was recorded some years later in an article on the school:

> In 1838 every coach was still on the road; mails also, five in number; the stage wagons containing the heavy merchandise of trade, drawn by six or eight horses, still going; carriers' carts and vans innumerable still plied on their busy errands.

Flocks of sheep with their clouds of dust, and droves of panting bullocks for the London Market were still driven by the drovers with their noisy dogs to Old Smithfield, and the high-road generally wore a scene of animation from early dawn to dewy eve. Boys might be seen wending their way from Hoddesdon, Wormley and Broxbourne to the well-known Old School. The entrance then was at the south-west corner where stood an old post, over which most boys thought it their duty to play leap-frog, and here it was the early boys were to be found playing at marbles, or swinging on the posts and chains in front of the "Harps" close by.[68]

For William, Paddington was quite possibly a convenient place to live, in terms of his journey to work. One of the first regular omnibus services ran from Paddington along the New Road. We might imagine William dismounting at the top of what is now Great Portland Street. He would be in Nash territory. The Regency period saw the crafting of Regent's Park and Regent Street North and South with their fine stucco buildings, whilst the Quadrant of Regent Street South carefully avoided the poorer streets of Soho. These fine architectural initiatives created enduring beauty, but displaced many thousands of poorer people who crowded ever more densely around the Strand. A further feature of London in the 1820s was the gas lighting of streets, which was spreading and would be largely complete by the 1840s.[69] William would have turned left to head for Great Marlborough Street and the premises occupied by Hullmandel in the haven for artists that was, and indeed is, Soho.

William's exact role, during his seventeen years with Hullmandel, we don't know, but it is clear from a paper that he presented to the Society of Arts on 22 December 1847 that he had a command of most aspects of the business. More remarkable though, was the provenance of the paper. Sir Henry Cole, sometime chairman of the Society, was a great champion of the common good. A firm adherent of the Benthamite doctrine of the greatest happiness of the greatest number, he championed projects as diverse as the Penny Post, a common gauge for railways, and improvements in sewerage disposal.[70] It was Cole who worked with William on the preparation of the paper. Cole wanted to promote good book design and production and he encouraged a series of papers on different aspects of printing. That he chose William for the paper on lithography is surely evidence of the high regard in which he was held and his ability to write.

This regard came through his employment by Hullmandel, but also and, possibly more so, through his writings for periodicals such as *The Spectator*, *The Athenaeum* and *The Examiner*. Cole's biography, entitled *The Great Exhibitor*, records his friendship with the then editor of *The Athenaeum*, for which he was also a contributor[71]. It is, surely, more than possible that Cole and William struck up a friendship. Having said this, Cole was said to be a man of boundless energy who relished a large audience. We might wonder at just how he got on with William whom the many Brontë biographies see as quiet and unassuming.

A survey of the paper *On Lithography*, which William presented, will help in appreciating the broad scope of his knowledge and understanding.[72] The Society had collected a large number of examples of the art for view by members.

By kind permission of the Royal Society of Arts

William begins his paper by making two points. First, the wide variety demonstrated by the examples exhibited, but, second, the rapid progress which had been made since the first discovery some fifty years earlier. He then recites the story of the discovery by Aloys Senefelder and explains how it was brought to England by Hullmandel. He then describes the various techniques, before moving onto ground that seems to be closer to his heart: the artists. The first English proponents, he says, were William Nicholson and the distinguished water-colourists Samuel Prout and J.D. Harding.

The mention of Samuel Prout draws in the name of John Ruskin for two reasons. First, whilst Ruskin seems to have been much in favour of traditional engraving, his biographer tells how, at a young age he encountered Hullmandel's skills and, quite possibly, met William.[73] The year was 1833 and Prout had, with Hullmandel, produced a volume of *Sketches in Flanders and Germany*. James Ruskin had subscribed to the edition, and father and son went to Great Marlborough Street to collect their copy. The sketches so impressed them that they spent the next three weeks planning a trip to Flanders and Germany. The trip did not disappoint and indeed extended to Switzerland, Italy and France.

John Ruskin will appear a number of times in William's story and his works, thinking, achievements and aspirations will emerge. At this early stage it is probably sufficient to say that John was an only child, and very much the apple of his parents' eye. His father, James, was a partner in the sherry shipping firm of Peter Domecq, known in full as Ruskin, Telford and Domecq. It was said that 'Domecq supplied the sherry, Telford the capital and Ruskin the brains.[74]' Huxley, in his book *The House of Smith, Elder*, says of Ruskin's mother that she was absolutely without humour. She was also said to have been so concerned for her son that she took lodgings in Oxford when he gained his place at the university.

The second Ruskin link in William's paper is that in his book, *Modern Painters*, where Ruskin is most complimentary of Prout:

> We owe Prout, I believe, the first perception and certainly the only existing expression of precisely the characters which were wanting to old art; of that feeling which results from the influence, among the noble lines of architecture, of the rent and the rust, the fissure, the lichen and the weed, and from the writing upon the pages of ancient walls of the confused hieroglyphics of human history.[75]

In his paper, William says of Prout, '[his] vigorous and picturesque pencilling, and his broad effects of light and shade, are very effective on stone; and his facility and fertility are evidenced in innumerable studies, as well as larger works; such as his *Views on the Rhine*, and two volumes of Sketches. No artist has made better use of lithography than Samuel Prout, or has done more for art by this means'.[76] The Tate Gallery's biographical note on Prout tells that he was 'one of the masters of British watercolour architectural painting. Prout secured the position of Painter in Water-Colours in Ordinary to King George IV in 1829 and afterwards to Queen Victoria'. He had been born in Plymouth in 1783 and died in 1852.

However, it wasn't Prout who, for William, took lithography to an altogether different level. William cites critics as condemning lithography for lacking the precision of engraving, but then missing the point that artists, such as Harding produced finished pictures through lithography, 'admirable for their union of force and elegance of style and striking effects of chiaroscuro'. He goes on to say that the pubic also undervalued the 'rough freedom of Lithographic sketches'.[77] For William, it was through Richard Lane A.R.A. that lithography rose in public estimation with his 'highly finished drawings' and 'his exquisite miniature imitations of sketches by Gainsborough and Edwin Landseer'.[78]

In the context of William's own story, he cites Lowes Dickinson's 'faithful and spirited versions of George Richmond's inimitable portraits'.[79] Lowes Dickinson would become William's son-in-law when, on 15 October 1857, he married Ellen, William's eldest daughter on her thirty-first birthday. This is possibly the place to digress a little into the Dickinson family. Lowes Dickinson's father, Joseph, was in business in Bond Street as a stationer and seller of fine prints. This business developed into lithographic printing and, later, photography with Lowes going into partnership with his brothers William and Gilbert. A search of the National Portrait Gallery collection reveals a good number of collaborations between Hullmandel and Dickinson, interestingly often featuring Richard Lane as the artist. Lowes Dickinson, himself, was already making his way as a portrait painter. The *Dictionary of National Biography* tells how he featured in the Royal Academy Exhibition every year between 1848 and 1891, missing only 1849, 1853 and 1884. The years 1849 and 1853 may be explained by his absence in Italy learning his art. Among his better-known paintings are his 1862 portrait of *Charles Kingsley*, *The Three Founders of the I Zingari Cricket Club*, *Gladstone's Cabinet of 1868* and *George Eliot*. He will appear a number of times in William's story.

The Three Founders of I Zingari Cricket Club – Cato Lowes Dickinson

Returning to William's paper, he cites 'Gould's magnificent series of ornithological works [as] among the most attractive and costly contributions to the study of natural history'.[80] It would, arguably, be works of natural history that would lead to William's departure from Hullmandel; John Gould was the author of the volume on birds in Charles Darwin's five volume *Zoology of the Voyage of H.M.S. Beagle*, of which I will tell more later.

William sees a place for both engraving and for lithography. Lithography cannot 'match engraving for mezzotints of fine line engravings'. What it can do is reproduce, many times over, the original work of an artist and it is there that its great value lies. This surely, would have gained the wholehearted approval of Henry Cole. The paper continues by describing how lithography embraces colour, shading and the use of tints. William highlights the importance of the artist first understanding his subject, since drawing on stone is no more than 'manual dexterity'. He explains that chromolithography, as practiced by Owen Jones, has 'carried coloured printing to a such a pitch of perfection that its productions now emulate the Illuminated Missals of the middle-ages and the water-colour drawings of modern painters'.

A drawback of lithography is the need to reverse the writing or drawing. William describes the method of transfer as overcoming this, whereby the artist or calligrapher can produce the image or text as it will be reproduced. This is pressed on the stone and the mirror image imbibed. The result can then be reproduced at will. Another drawback, with large maps for example - is the sheer weight of the stone. Hullmandel developed a process whereby zinc is substituted for stone. A further development was known as the Anastatic Printing machine which William confidently stated would be up and running in London by the time the paper was presented. It was the forerunner of photocopying.

My purpose in drawing, at some length, from William's paper was to show that he was indeed very well versed in the techniques and application of lithography.

He was also beginning to assume the mantle of an encourager of young talent, for which he would later be well known. On 12 October 1840, Charles Dickens wrote to William to thank him for his congratulations contained in a letter written some six weeks earlier.[81] From April 1840, Dickens had been publishing *The Old Curiosity Shop* in instalments in a periodical called *Master Humphrey's Clock*. The letter closes with Dickens saying that he had written to Mr Sibson, whom William was clearly encouraging. Thomas Sibson had created a series of plates of scenes from Dickens's books.[82] His plates, dated 1840-42, illustrating *The Old Curiosity Shop* were published by Robert Tyas of Cheapside. Sibson was later described in *Pictorial Pickwickiana* as 'a youthful genius whose remarkable contributions are the least known'.

William's professional life had yet a further dimension: his regular contributions to periodicals. His obituary in *The Athenaeum* spoke of frequent contributions on literary, artistic and theatrical matters to the *Athenaeum, Spectator and Examiner*. All three magazines had editors with strong characters and strong views. Albany Fonblanque took over The *Examiner* from Leigh Hunt in 1828 and edited it until 1847. The editor of *The Spectator* from 1828 until his death in 1858 was Robert Rintoul. *The Athenaeum* was edited by Charles Dilke from 1828 to 1846. The authorship of pieces in periodicals of the time generally remained anonymous. One fortuitous exception is the case of *The Athenaeum* where, for a few years, the editor, Charles Dilke, annotated a number of contributions with the surnames of the authors. In 1842 and 1843, the name Williams appears on a number of occasions. Extracts from several of these offer a sense of William's style and breadth of interest. Much of the writing is on fine art: many of the articles are reviews and a number of these are surprisingly robust, but with a broad range in interests.

In a review of fine art in the final edition of 1842, William writes of lithography but also of a concern for educating the young - a theme that will recur in William's story.

> Roberts's *Sketches of the Holy Land* proceed in a manner to satisfy the subscribers both with the interest of the views and the finished execution of the lithography, by Mr Haghe. Parts V and VI illustrate the excavated temples and dwellings of Petra, showing the face of the rocky cliffs carved into the architectural forms of Greece; the facades enriched with sculptured figures and ornaments, and other ravines perforated with caves, the approaches to which not visible. The purity and evenness of the tints, the firmness of the outline, the solidity of the relief produced by

the raised lights, and the tender graduations of the half-tints, are points in the lithography worthy of admiration and imitation. The tenth part of Mr Brockedon's *Italy* enables us to report favourably of this *variorum* edition of Italian scenery; and the second part of a series of *Chronological Pictures of English History* designed and lithographed by Mr John Gilbert and exhibiting the leading events, the costume, architecture, &c of each monarch's reign on a separate sheet, makes us aware that artistic talent of no ordinary kind is engaged in teaching the young through the eye. A spirited and elegant sketch of *Sir Henry Pottinger* by Samuel Lawrence, lithographed by Lowes Dickinson, conveys an animated idea of the physiognomy of a bold and decided character; the likeness is one of that kind which carries conviction of its truth.[83]

Writing about a series of sketches which appeared under the title *Portraits of the Princes and People of India*, William says that 'the drawings are lithographed with tints and white lights by Mr Lowes Dickinson who has shown himself, by the skill and spirit with which he has rendered the coloured sketches into neutral tints of lithography, one of the first figure draughtsmen on stone'.[84] A further piece from 8 April also has its focus on lithography:

The volumes of lithographic sketches put forth by favourite artists beginning with Prout, Harding and Stanfield, and coming down to Nash, Haghe, and Roberts - are exclusively of a popular character; their attractiveness consisting either in the charm of the style, the picturesque nature of the subjects, or the interest attached to the scenes delineated: with the exception of Mr Gally Knight's architectural illustrations of 'The Normans in Sicily', no single one of the numerous series makes pretensions to archaeological research. In proportion as we regret this deficiency of exact information and scientific character, should we welcome the appearance of a work which combines pictorial beauty with learned investigation, and is that once valuable to the architectural student and acceptable to the lovers of art.[85]

In the edition of 11 May 1843, William turns his attention to new publications:

> The publishing season has commenced with what looks like unusual activity after the stagnant state into which the print trade had subsided.
>
> Foremost in magnitude and pretensions, though not in interest or excellence, is Mr Ryle's elaborate engraving after Sir George Hayter's clever composition, but vulgar picture, of *The Coronation of Queen Victoria*. The arrangement of the groups and the general effect of the scene are good, but the figures remind one of Madame Tussaud's waxwork and the Royal and noble personages look with smirking meaningless stare, as if waiting for some signal to show that enthusiasm which ought to burst forth spontaneously, and characterise the very moment - the act of Coronation being just accomplished. The immense character of the chin of almost every face is an extraordinary peculiarity and there is an expression about the mouth of each as if the jaw were, what is termed, underhung.[86]

A journey through *The Athenaeum* magazine is akin to a journey through the intellectual life of the nation, for in the edition of 18 August 1843, there is a report on the thirteenth meeting of the British Association for the Advancement of Science. Elsewhere, art and science sit comfortably as stablemates.

On the subject of theatre being made more readily available William writes on 21 October:

> If the mountain will not go to Mohammed, Mohammed must go to the mountain; instead of having half a dozen theatres in the space of the square mile round Covent Garden, let the suburbs each have their playhouse, as well as their concert and assembly rooms - orchestras are ambulatory to a certain extent and musicians are migratory; why not make Melpomene locomotive and revive the thespian cast in the shape of an actors' omnibus with a managerial conductor. At all events, since the old English Drama is driven from Drury Lane and Covent Garden, let us hope it will find a home somewhere else. One good result of the new Act may be to lodge Shakespeare under a roof where his poetry may be heard without being bawled out "as if the town crier spoke the lines", and actors may depict the emotions of his characters without distorting the features to make the grimaces visible at the house tops: in short a better school of acting may arise if the best performers are in the habit of playing together on a small stage.[87]

A further piece on theatre on 28 October finds William's sharper pen aimed at farce:

> The only new pieces have been furnished by the well-known manufacturer of British Dramas and translator of foreign farces, Mr Maddison Morton, who within a few days has had three fresh fun-making machines at work; one at each of the principal theatres. Harley at Drury Lane, Keeley at Covent Garden, and Buckstone at the Haymarket, assisted by their respective crews, exerted their mirth-producing powers to the

utmost and managed to get up the steam of merriment; but neither of the three engines of drollery is likely to run any length of time, though one is started on a French railroad constructed after a Parisien model. This comparison of a farce to a piece of machinery is neither so far-fetched nor infelicitous as would seem at first sight - at least not in this case; for the fun-making apparatus is so cumbrous and complicated and works so mechanically - though requiring a number of persons to set it in motion and constant labour to keep it going - there is such a continual noise and bustle of people running to and fro, and shouting, and such desperate efforts required to overcome the resisting force of gravity in the audience, owing to the small supply of unctuous humour, that the simile may perhaps be allowed.[88]

On the subject of monuments and memorials, William writes just two days before Christmas:

> This is not a poetical age; fitting emblems are few, and not very intelligible: a flower snapped from the stalk is almost the only graceful and expressive emblem of youth and innocence. In the Kensal Green Cemetery is a tomb with a dead lamb sculpted on it, which, besides looking unsightly, awakens ideas of the shambles; and we remember to have seen a dead bird which at once carries you to the poulterer's. The broken column is not so bad but these, and all similar emblems, are anything but hopeful. The Greeks symbolised the soul by a butterfly; we, in this material age, typify the soul in a bodily form. If it will wish to express the changes the mortal part of us undergoes after death, our scientific notions might suggest a retort and receiver. Not being a

poetical people, we are, therefore, incompetent either to invent or understand symbols, and it would be best to avoid them altogether.[89]

I have already referred to reports on science sitting comfortably alongside the arts. In addition, each periodical contained space for the political and social issues of the day. By reading them, William would have been thoroughly well informed. He would also be well informed simply by having his eyes open to the London surrounding his daily life. The Select Committee on Metropolis Improvements reported this in 1836:

> There are some districts in this vast city through which no great thoroughfares pass, and which, being wholly occupied by a population composed of the lowest class of labourers, entirely secluded from the observation and influence of wealthier and better educated neighbours, exhibit a state of moral and physical degradation deeply to be deplored[…] The moral condition of these poorer occupants must necessarily be improved by immediate communication with a more respectable inhabitancy; and the introducing at the same time of improved habits and free circulation of air will tend materially to extirpate those prevalent diseases which are now not only so destructive amongst themselves, but so dangerous to the neighbourhood around them.[90]

In the early 1840s, three works were published which cast a light on these terrible conditions in which a great many of William's fellow Britons were living.[91] *The Examiner* of 29 April 1843 contained a long and positive review of Carlyle's *Past and Present,* which was a strong condemnation of the adverse impact of industrialisation on the condition of ordinary people. *The Athenaeum* reviewed the book in its edition of 20 May. This work came only a year after the publication of Edwin Chadwick's Report on the *Sanitary Condition of the Labouring Population of Great Britain*. Two years later *Sybil, or The Two Nations,* by the young Benjamin Disraeli, would draw the attention of a Tory audience to conditions from which they were far removed. For many in William's position, there was little that could be done to address these issues without the vote.

William's family moved in 1833 from Paddington to Kentish Town - an area of new housing then on the edge of the growing metropolis. They lived at 25 and then 31 Harmood Street which runs between Chalk Farm Road and Prince of Wales Road, to the north of Regent's Park. I visited Harmood Street hoping to find, from looking at the houses, that the family was 'moving up in the world'. Sadly, the side of the street with odd numbers in the 20s and 30s now had new town houses, however on the other side there remains a delightful row of small late Georgian terraced houses. The family's move coincided with the passing, after much fierce argument both in and out of Parliament, of the first Reform Act which extended the franchise to more male holders of freehold property. I searched the London electoral register to find William's name. It didn't appear until 1867, when the family was living in Twickenham. The franchise had, by then, been extended by the second Reform Act of 1867 to include more of those renting, rather than owning houses. I find myself shocked that a man of William's intelligence had to wait most of his life before getting the vote. It is, of course no more shocking than the fact that few, if any, of the women mentioned in this volume ever got to exercise their democratic rights at the ballot box. The long hard battle to secure votes for women was, though, gathering steam during William's life.

William's family grew again, first with the birth of Robert Henry on 13 October 1837 (the year the young Victoria came to the throne) and then Richard Smith on 29 July 1839. I can find no record of baptisms for either Robert or Richard. There are all sorts of possible reasons for this, the first being incomplete records and my own shortcomings in research. However, the whole question of the Established Church and religion was very much up in the air in most of the nineteenth century. In the Church of England there was a struggle. At the High Church end of the spectrum, there were those who espoused the Oxford Movement and inspired the architecture of the Gothic Revival. At the Low Church end, the idea of Muscular Christianity was being promoted by Christian socialists such as F.D. Maurice. Evangelical adherence to scripture had a strong following, and Methodism was gaining ground, particularly in urban areas. The 1830s saw the coming of Catholic emancipation. Yet, atheism was becoming acceptable. Certainly, the influence of people like Leigh Hunt and John Taylor would have led William's thinking away from established religion. William's religious views emerge rather more in his correspondence with Charlotte Brontë, as we will see later.

Between 1841 and 1843, the family lived in Vicarage Place, Kensington and it was here that Thornton Arthur was born. Margaret Smith notes that Leigh Hunt lived at 32 Edwardes Square, Kensington and that it was possibly during this time that the families became friends.[92] The name Thornton had also been given by Leigh Hunt to his son; this is perhaps a further indication of their friendship. I can find no record of Thornton Arthur's baptism until he became an adult.

When I think of Vicarage Place, Kensington (just off what is now Kensington High Street), to be honest, I think 'smart London'. A piece from the 1850s brought me sharply back:

> The Rookery has long been a nuisance in Kensington. In the morning you seldom see more of it than this indication at the entrance; but in the evening the inmates mingle with the rest of the inhabitants out of doors, and the naked feet of children, and the ragged and dissolute looks of men and women, present a painful contrast to the general decency. We understand, however, that some of these poor people are very respectable of their kind, and that the improvements which are taking place in other portions of the kingdom, in late years to the destitute and uneducated, have not been without effect in this quarter. The men for the most part are, or profess to be, labouring bricklayers, and the women market-garden women. They are calculated, at a rough guess, to amount to a thousand; all crammed, perhaps, into a place

which ought not to contain above a hundred. Most of this unhappy multitude are Roman Catholics.[93]

William was, thus, very far from separated from the hardships faced by many at that time. His professional story was about to take a change in direction. The passage written by George Smith (junior) in his memoirs, recalling how William came to join Smith, Elder & Co., described William as a not-very-good bookkeeper who was utterly fed up with his work at Hullmandel. This might well have been true then, but, as we have seen, William had been a great deal more than simply a bookkeeper; he had observed, learnt and offered critique. A letter from Charles Darwin perhaps sheds a little light on quite why William chose to change his employment. It is dated 11 March 1844, addressed to his close friend and colleague J.D. Hooker, and concerns the printing of illustrations by the firm of lithographers who had done so for the for his *Zoology of the Voyage of HMS Beagle*. He makes two quite contrasting remarks about William's future and current employers:

> I have found Smith & Elder a most pleasant, fair, attentive, & obliging firm to have any business with.
>
> I know that an artist can almost immediately learn to draw on Lithographic stones. I believe Hullmandel is a good Lithog. printer; but I found him rather troublesome.[94]

William had perhaps heard Darwin speak of his publisher in glowing terms and quite possibly Charles Hullmandel was becoming a rather troublesome employer, not least if he was requiring William to work in a position to which he was unsuited?

4 THE HOUSE OF SMITH, ELDER

William would spend over thirty years (more than half his profession life) in what would be called The House of Smith & Elder. But what kind of publishing house was it? By the time he joined, it had been active for some thirty years.

The publishing house, Smith, Elder & Co., had been founded in 1816 by George Smith (senior) and Alexander Elder as booksellers and stationers.[95] George Smith was born in Elgin and served his apprenticeship in Scotland before joining the large numbers of ambitious young men seeking their fortune in London. Smith began with Rivington's, but he soon moved to one of the largest publishing houses of the time, John Murray which would, over a century later, become owner of the publishing house that Smith created.[96]

The early publishing output of Smith, Elder & Co. included the annual *Friendship's Offering*. In his book *The House of Smith Elder,* Leonard Huxley describes its contributors as 'writers of established reputation, ladies of quality and beginners destined to achieve fame' and they included Coleridge, Tennyson and

Clare, perhaps taking up the baton put down when Taylor and Hessey parted company.[97] They published a number of good-quality books of illustrations including some thirty-five views of Scottish towns, and a series of romantic novels. They moved into the publishing of the work of naturalists - ultimately, as we have seen, Charles Darwin's *Zoology of the Voyage of HMS Beagle,* and *Results of Astronomical Observations Made During the years 1834-8 at the Cape of Good Hope* by Sir John Herschel.

As required, in order to be a publishing house, both partners had been admitted to the Stationers' Company in 1819. But it was more. It was a bookshop selling both new and second-hand titles. It also sold quality stationery and all from the premises it moved to in 1824 at 65 Cornhill, owned by the Grocers' Company at the entrance to White Lion Court.[98] It built a considerable agency and banking business with India which would, over the years, demand attention from the owners, distracting them from their publishing activity.

It was on 19 March 1824 that George Smith (junior) was born to Elizabeth Murray, whom George (senior) had married in 1820. Elizabeth would go on to have a major role in supporting her son in running the company after her husband's death. Following a sickly childhood and a disappointing school career, George Smith (junior) entered the business as an apprentice in 1838, just as it began the publication of Sir Humphry Davy's *Works.*[99] For the next seven years, Smith would work in nearly all parts of the business, not least those many aspects connected with India. In his autobiography, Smith recalls his time as an apprentice. He was at work from 7.30a.m. until 8.00p.m., but with time off during the afternoon to learn to ride. In terms of his duties, he would do anything from mending the office quill pens to learning how to bind books and compose type.[100] It would not be unreasonable to suppose that William's own apprenticeship had included such practical tasks.

In 1843, Smith (junior) was given £1,500 to invest in new publications.[101] He had been placed in charge of the publishing department of the firm and he rose to the challenge with great enthusiasm. His first venture was the publication of RH *'Orion'* Horne's *A New Spirit of the Age*. In this book Horne, assisted by Elizabeth Barrett Browning, offers pieces by many of the great writers of the age including Carlyle and, significantly for us, Charles Wells's poem *Joseph and His Brethren*. Horne's book was read by those most concerned with the literature of the day, including Dante Gabriel Rossetti. Theodore Watts-Dunton explains that Rossetti was so taken with the notice about Wells's poem that he made straight away for the British Museum, where he read the poem in full and pronounced that it was 'more Shakespearean than anything else out of Shakespeare'.[102] Rossetti showed the poem to a number of 'men of genius' including Mr Swinburne, who wrote an essay on it for Fraser's Magazine. Sadly, the essay was not published and so, Watts-Dunton records, *Joseph and His Brethren* 'had thirteen years more in the dust-bin'. It will, though, re-emerge in William's story.

Leonard Huxley offers two further anecdotes concerning Horne's book. The first was a piece by Horne on Colonel Perronet Thompson that contained views Smith thought 'not in the least likely to commend themselves to the book-buying public'. There followed a delightfully theatrical encounter at Horne's house in Kentish Town, at the end of which Horne threw the offending part of the manuscript into the fireplace. The second was that Thackeray reviewed the book for *The Morning Chronicle* 'on the whole favourably'.[103] William Makepeace Thackeray is a name that will recur many times in William's story.

Another of Smith's early publications was *Imagination and Fancy,* a collection of the best of English poetry, by Leigh Hunt. Huxley tells how Smith visited Hunt at his home in Kensington, how he heard Hunt's daughter sing on a number of occasions and how a sequence of further publications soon followed.[104] He also offers an anecdote about Hunt's wife. It seems that she had thrown into the fire an envelope of bank notes which Hunt had carelessly flung down. With Smith's evidence, the Bank of England replaced the lost notes.[105]

Elder was the partner with the greater interest in art, but in 1845 he retired from the partnership. A year later, on 21 August, George Smith (senior) died. This left the running of the business to Smith (junior) and the manager of the Indian branch. The strain on the young Smith was immense. If the running of the businesses was not enough, Smith also discovered that the manager responsible for the Indian business had been 'misusing the firms credit and capital'.[106] The crisis facing the firm demanded of the young Smith both excessive hours of work and great diplomatic skills to ensure that confidence in the firm didn't suffer. It seemed that, however much Smith might have loved the publishing side of the business, he needed to concentrate on India and the finances. He needed help from someone with great literary judgement.

William's obituary in *The Publishers' Circular* suggests that it was through John Ruskin that he met George Smith. The connection didn't seem obvious, and so I had to explore further. I found that, in the 1830s, John Ruskin's father, James. had offered Smith, Elder & Co. a series of verses by a Graduate of Oxford, which was duly published.[107] I wondered at how such an unknown quantity had managed to secure a publisher. Further research revealed that James Ruskin's cousin, Charles Richardson, worked for Smith, Elder & Co. and so could ease the passage to publication.[108] Notwithstanding this, in 1843, James Ruskin first approached the much more prestigious John Murray with a new volume then entitled *Turner and the Ancients*. Murray declined even to read it, and so Ruskin approached Smith, Elder & Co. who duly published it under the title *Modern Painters*. John Ruskin had affirmed his place in the Smith, Elder & Co. universe, and this time he took the art world by storm. This revolutionary book turned on its head much of the accepted thinking about painting. Ruskin had had the audacity to write warmly of Turner, whilst being rather dismissive of many of the great painters of the past.

William's own significant interest in art makes it worth taking a step back to try to see just what it was that Ruskin was saying. Timothy Hilton, writing about the *Pre-Raphaelite Brotherhood*, which Ruskin would energetically support, tells how Ruskin himself came to regard his own practice of painting. He explains how, at a young age, Ruskin had mastered the styles of both the major and minor artists of the day. Then, in 1842, on the road from Norwood to Peckham, all became clear. Of this revelation, Ruskin wrote in his autobiography *Praeterita*:

> I made, by sheer accident, my first drawing of leafage and natural growth - a few ivy leaves around a stump in a hedgerow[....]I never imitated anyone after that sketch was made; but entered at once upon the course of study that enabled me afterwards to understand Pre-Raphaelitism.[109]

I have already referred to reviews that William was writing for *The Athenaeum* in 1843. In the edition of 3 February 1844, there is a long review of *Modern Painters*. Scathing puts it lightly. The reviewer, who this time Dilke does not name, is clearly shocked by Ruskin's criticism of the great masters and his praise for Turner. At one point he says:

> The chief purpose of the writer was to heap terms of abuse and derision and disdain upon the

Old Masters often fulfilled with a verve and glibness as if the author had been a graduate of Billingsgate instead of Oxford.

He begins though in language not designed to soothe:

There is too much reasoning in this book without the higher qualities of reasoning, which are clearness and conclusiveness, subordination of parts, and able summation of the whole: perhaps we should have said too much parade of logic and too little real power. Yet it is a clever book neither - less nor more. It exhibits what may recommend it to many readers, some characteristics of Hazlitt's style – boldness and brilliance, bigotry amidst liberality, and great acuteness amid still greater blindness. Whether the author be an Oxford graduate or no, he appears beyond doubt an undergraduate in criticism, a very freshman; sanguine and self-confident, he would cut the Gordian knot with a bulrush, like one of those ambitious youths which undertake the trisection of an angle, or the duplication of the cube while they are still tingling from the schoolmaster's rod, and have scarce surmounted the *pons asinorum.*

William and Ruskin must have discussed the book and the review. Ruskin features more than once in Charlotte Brontë's letters to William. For example, her letter of 31 July 1848 speaks at length about how much she valued Ruskin's writing on Turner in *Modern Painters,* which William had sent to her in one of the parcels of books that arrived regularly in Haworth from Smith, Elder & Co.[110] The reviews may not have been complimentary, but they and others served to kick-start Ruskin's career. They also furthered William's own relationship with, and admiration for, Ruskin.

William joined Smith, Elder & Co. in 1845 and George Smith gave, in his memoirs, his account of the meeting with William that led to this. He explains first that Smith, Elder & Co.'s account with the firm of Hullmandel & Co was in a 'hopeless state of confusion'.[111]

> I went to see the bookkeeper of the firm of lithographers - Mr W Smith Williams - taking with me a bundle of accounts with a view to getting them arranged in proper form. Mr Williams gifts as a bookkeeper, I soon found, were of a most primitive character. I asked him how he had struck his numerous balances, remarking that we had no corresponding balances in our books.
>
> "Oh", said Mr Williams, "those are the bottoms of the pages in our ledger. I always strike a balance at the bottom of the page to avoid the necessity of carrying over the figures on both sides."
>
> I had a good many interviews with Mr Williams and, if he was not a good bookkeeper, he was a most agreeable and most intelligent man with literary gifts wasted in uncongenial work. My sympathy was excited by seeing one of so much ability occupied with work he did ill and which was distasteful to him; and by noticing the overbearing manner in which he was treated by the junior member of the firm which employed him.
>
> Mr Williams confided to me that, by way of relief from his bookkeeping efforts, he contributed reviews and other articles to *The Spectator,* then making its high position under the able editorship of Mr Rintoul. Mr Williams used also to write theatrical criticism for *The Spectator,* but found

himself hampered a good deal, he said, by the chilly temperament of his editor, Mr Rintoul, who used to say, in the most impressive manner, "The Spectator is not enthusiastic and must not be."

I fancied I had discovered the man who could help me and my publishing business. I invited Mr Williams to tea at my lodgings in Regent Street and after tea I said to him, "Rightly or wrongly I do not think you like your present occupation."

"I hate it," said Mr Williams with fervour.

This reply made clear sailing for me and before he left my room we had arranged that he should come to Cornhill as my literary assistant and general manager of the publishing department.

I do take issue with Smith's rather dismissive review of William's life up to that point, although it is clear from Charlotte Brontë's letters that William, too, felt dissatisfied. I just think that what we have seen in his writing on lithography and art more generally speaks of a cultured, intelligent and able man. I also add a note of amusement, as, when I examined the family tree, I saw a disproportionate number of accountants who could trace their ancestry to William. George Smith (junior) would pursue a glittering career in publishing; the title of his biography by Jenifer Glyn says it all: *Prince of Publishers*. He would publish possibly most of the nineteenth century's greatest authors writing in the English language. Surely, a good part of this success he must owe to his Reader

In 1844, the Williams family had moved from Kensington to 3 Campden Hill Terrace (now 98 Campden Hill Road), where critic George Henry Lewes, his wife and family were to be their neighbours for the next three years.

William and Lewes had many professional interests in common. Their relationship did, though, have another dimension. Academic Franklin Gary, writing in 1936, draws his readers' attention to mention of a circle of which William and Lewes seem to have been a part. A number of books on Lewes and Leigh Hunt's son, Thornton Hunt, speak of a phalanstery - a group of men and women living together, following the inspiration of the French socialist, Fourier and novelist George Sand. This group was said to be based at a house in Queen's Road Bayswater, and this attracted scandalous attention; the sources, however, do not agree on whether Lewes ever lived there.

The evidence of William being part of the wider intellectual circle comes from novelist Eliza Lynn Linton, who wrote of her own visits to the circle. Franklin Gary quotes her as characterising William as:

> A man who fulfilled the Spanish proverb about him who speaks softly and writes harshly. In voice, manner and conversation, he was the gentlest creature imaginable; but his letters were harsh and acrid, and no one could think more cruelly than he - no one wound more deeply when it came to pen and ink in contradiction of his mild words and half hinted promises.[112]

Franklin Gary adds:

> I cannot help wondering if the novel of Mrs Lynn Linton had been rejected by the reader of Smith, Elder and Co. It is only fair to say that Charlotte Brontë's letters lead one to form a somewhat different opinion of this man whom she described to her friend Mary Taylor in a letter of 4 September 1848 as "a pale mild stooping man of fifty very much like a faded Tom Dixon".[113]

William was certainly capable of saying no. He read Catherine Spence's *Clara Morison* but declined it with a letter similar to that he sent to Charlotte Brontë on reading *The Professor,* which I will explore in the next chapter.[114] I might add, from reading his articles, that William was certainly capable of sharp critique, but the overall impression is surely that held by Charlotte and, indeed, many others as evidenced by those words I quoted from his obituary in *The Athenaeum*.

The Williams and Lewes families would also develop a close relationship. The Leweses had four sons: Charles Lee (1842-91), Thornton Arnott (1844-69), Herbert Arthur (1846-75) and St Vincent Arthy (1848-50). Gordon Haight, in his biography of George Eliot (with whom Wells subsequently would have a longstanding relationship), explains that Charles was born when they lived at 3 Pembroke Square in Kensington, Thornton at 2 Campden Hill Terrace and the others when they had moved to 26 Bedford Place where the Lewes lived from 1848 to 1855. This, he explains, refutes the suggestion that they may have lived at the phalanstery.[115] As for William, there is no evidence at all that he did, indeed all the evidence points to him being the head of a very strong family. William's son Richard, writing after the death of his sister Anna in the 1920s, is at pains to stress the presence of Lewes in the lives of the Williams family not least that two of their sons, Charles Lee and Thornton Arnott went to the same school as he did in Bayswater.[116]

William's relationship with Thornton Hunt and George Lewes would extend over many years. The Lewes and Hunt families would, though, later undergo a degree of change, with George Lewes leaving his wife and spending the rest of his life 'unmarried' to George Eliot. I tell more of this in Chapter 8.

William's desk would have on it the manuscripts sent in by aspiring authors. We know, from the introduction to Ruskin's Complete Works, that volume II of *Modern Painters* followed the first in 1846. Some ten years would elapse before the third and fourth volumes were published together, and a further four years before the fifth and final volume in 1860. After the publication of the second volume of *Modern Painters,* Ruskin turned his attention to architecture and, in 1849, he produced *The Seven Lamps of Architecture.* The first volume of *The Stones of Venice* followed in 1851, accompanied by *Examples of the Architecture of Venice* and then, in 1853, by the second and third volumes of *The Stones of Venice.* All this work came through the offices of Smith, Elder & Co.

Theodore Watts-Dunton tells that, around 1845, Charles Wells submitted to Smith, Elder & Co. an historical romance whose title would have struck a distant chord, *Gaston de Blondeville.* He tells that William thought highly of it, but that it lacked 'that something without which no novel can find a market'.

William would have overseen, in 1846 and the early part of 1847, the publication of a number of the novels of GPR James, which Smith's father had taken on and which were growing less popular. He might also have been involved in the publication of *The Queen of the Stage* by Mrs Baron Wilson and, in all probability, oversaw the continuing publication of Leigh Hunt's poems.

William's youngest daughter, Anna, was born in Campden Hill Terrace in 1845. Many years later, she spoke in an interview of the Smith Williams family household. She had, by then, become a celebrated soprano. Her interviewer wrote that 'Mr Smith Williams was a man of an extreme romantic and artistic temperament. In the evening the small petted Anna would sit on a stool at his knee while he said to the older ones - "Now, girls, shall we have some Mozart?" "I don't like Mozart!" the little maiden would say. "Can't we have some operatic music instead?" But Mozart invariably carried the day.' There is a description of the Williams household from some three years later when William Rossetti visited. He recalled 'a very large family in a very small house'[117](now 98 Campden Hill Road).

Norman Penty confirmed this when he visited the house whilst he was researching his *Genealogical Quest*. He writes:

> In the Williams' time there would have been an entrance hall and two ground floor rooms, one being the parlour/sitting room entered from the hall, with possibly folding doors opening into a dining room at the back, which leads out to an iron veranda with steps leading down to the small neat garden. On each of the first and top floors there would probably have been two bedrooms with the children having to share sleeping

facilities. In the large basement would have been found the kitchen, pantry, coal room with an entry hole from the front pavement above, and possibly a bedroom for a servant. A water closet was situated outside at garden level.[118]

William's, and indeed his wife's, caring natures is revealed when, in February 1847, the already crowded house squeezed in, perhaps, two further occupants: Julia Kavanagh and her mother Bridget. Julia was a young Irish writer and Eileen Fauset suggests that 'it is possible that Kavanagh and her mother lodged with the Williamses for a period of four months before finding permanent lodgings in Allison Terrace".[119] Her correspondence address was given as 3 Campden Terrace from 27 February to 9 August 1847. Faucet goes on to say that a number of William's letters to Charlotte Brontë suggest that the families shared a sense of warmth and trust. Julia Kavanagh was the only child of Morgan and Bridget Kavanagh, born in Ireland on on 7 January 1824. She had arrived in London in 1844 having spent her childhood and youth in France. Her parents separated in 1847, and Julia and her mother would live together until Julia's death in 1877. Julia set to and succeeded in earning her living through her writing which she did in a quiet, unassuming and effective way. She wrote some fourteen known novels aimed at a domestic market, she contributed to a number of women's journals, she wrote pamphlets and a number of biographical works, including *Women in France During the Eighteenth Century* and *English Women of Letters*.[120] Julia Kavanagh is another writer who will appear more than once in William's story.

In 1847, I think it is fair to say, that William has found, or had found for him, a job thoroughly suited to his very particular talents but also to his character.

5 BRONTË YEARS – JANE EYRE

On a July day in 1847, William was at his desk at 65 Cornhill, no doubt contemplating what the new day might bring. The young George Smith entered his small office with an unprepossessing parcel: a manuscript which had already been turned down by a competitor - the readdressed package being an all-too-obvious clue. In the light of this, it is a wonder, then, that the package actually ended up on William's desk at all. It did, but it was destined to remain unread all day. It was to 3 Campden Hill Terrace, noisy with eight children, that William returned home that evening, clutching the package which, he discovered, contained the manuscript of *The Professor*, by one Currer Bell.

William had been with Smith, Elder & Co. for just two years, but he was respected and Smith was confident in his literary judgement. William read the manuscript with his accustomed care, quite unaware of the true identity of the author and, indeed, only able to assume that it was the work of an unknown male writer. Nevertheless, he recommended to George Smith that, whilst the book was not suitable for publication, the author should be encouraged to submit a further work for their consideration. He wrote to Bell. Charlotte Brontë, using her nom de plume of Currer Bell, replied thus on 7 August 1847:

> I have received your communication of the 5th inst. for which I thank you.
>
> Your objection to the want of varied interest in the tale, is, I am aware, not without grounds - yet it appears that it might be published without serious risk if its appearance were speedily followed up by another work from the same pen of a more striking and exciting character. The first work might serve as an introduction and accustom the public to the author's name, the success of the second might thereby be rendered more probable.
>
> I have a second narrative in 3 vols now in progress and nearly completed, to which I have endeavoured to impart a more vivid interest than belongs to the Professor; in about a month I hope to finish it - so that if a publisher were found for "the Professor", the second narrative might follow as soon as was deemed advisable - and thus the interest of the public (if any interests were roused) might not be suffered to cool.
>
> Will you be kind enough to favour me with your judgement of this plan?
>
> I am Gentlemen, yours very respectfully, C Bell[121]

The second narrative, *Jane Eyre*, duly arrived with Smith Elder & Co. on 24 August 1847. We do not know how William reacted when the parcel containing the manuscript of *Jane Eyre* arrived. Possibly it was with amusement, since with it there was a note saying:

I find I cannot prepay the carriage on the parcel, as money for that purpose is not received at the small station where it is left. If, when you acknowledge receipt of the parcel, you would have the goodness to mention the amount charged on delivery, I will immediately transmit ii in postage-stamps.[122]

It seems that William asked a more junior reader to take the manuscript first. George Smith recalled that this young reader was so powerfully struck by the tale that his enthusiasm caused merriment: 'You seem to have been so enchanted, that I do not know how to believe you.' William was a more clear-headed judge, yet he admitted to staying up all night to finish the manuscript. We have no record of his wife or children's reactions. George Smith recalled his own reaction in an autobiographical piece included in his memoirs:

> [William] brought it to me on a Saturday, and said that he would like me to read it. There were no Saturday half-holidays in those days, and as usual, I did not reach home until late. I had made an appointment with a friend for Sunday morning; I was to meet him about twelve o'clock at a place some two or three miles from our house, and ride with him into the country.
>
> After breakfast on Sunday morning I took the [manuscript] of "Jane Eyre" to my little study, and began to read it. The story quickly took me captive. Before twelve o'clock my horse came to the door, but I could not put the book down. I scribbled two or three lines to my friend, saying that I was very sorry that circumstances had arisen to prevent my meeting him, set the note off by my groom, and went on reading the [manuscript]. Presently the servant came to

tell me that luncheon was ready; I asked him to bring me a sandwich and a glass of wine, and still went on with "Jane Eyre". Dinner came; for me the meal was a very hasty one, and before I went to bed that night I had finished reading the manuscript.[123]

It is appropriate to pause at this point to see the actual extent of George Smith's enthusiasm, but also to recognise just how revolutionary *Jane Eyre* was.

As to the first, Juliet Barker points out that 'the terms on which it was published were not overly generous, even for a first-time author. Currer Bell was offered one hundred pounds for the copyright on the condition that Smith, Elder & Co. had the first right of refusal to his next two books, for which he was also to receive one hundred pounds each'.[124]

Turning to the second, I doubt that many would question the genius of Jane Austen, who was writing some thirty years earlier; indeed, William later encouraged Charlotte to read her work and perhaps to learn from her. Jane Austen had held up a mirror at the governing classes so that they could see just how ridiculous, on occasions, they were. Charlotte Brontë, however, did the unthinkable - she created a strong female protagonist who had the audacity to question established behaviour. Given William's exposure to radical views aired in the well-known periodicals, but also encountered thus far in his career, it is perhaps not surprising that he would see huge merit in a work such as *Jane Eyre*. Perhaps having a wife of strong character and four intelligent daughters might also have attracted him to Jane's character. I wonder too whether Charlotte's gentle critique of certain religious practices and beliefs might have struck a chord with William.

David Cannadine in his wide-ranging view of the United Kingdom from 1800 to 1906, *Victorious Century*, has this to say about the Brontës in the context of their critique of society:

Many of the publications that poured from the presses during the second half of the [1840s] were[...]wide ranging in their pronunciation is of the ills of contemporary Britain. Charlotte Brontë in *Jane Eyre* and her sister Emily in *Wuthering Heights* both 1847 offered trenchant critiques of gender relations, patriarchal society and class inequality.[125]

Cannadine places these books in the same bracket as the other great novelists of the 19th century literary scene when he writes:

> Charles Dickens *Dombey and Son* (1848) denounced child cruelty and arranged marriages for financial gain. Charles Kingsley's *Yeast* (1848) was equally critical of the social system that condemned so many agricultural labourers to poverty. Elizabeth Gaskell's *Mary Barton* (1848) drew renewed attention to the plight of the industrial working class in Manchester. In *Vanity Fair* (1848) and *Pendennis* (1848 to 1850), William Makepeace Thackeray assailed greed, idleness, snobbery, deceit and hypocrisy that he believed was so marked among the upper classes.

It wasn't only through fiction that criticism of contemporary society was being voiced as Cannadine explains by surveying the works of John Stuart Mill, Kingsley and Ruskin.

William read the manuscript at the end of August. We can infer (and it has to be inference since William's letters sadly appear to have been lost) that he wrote to Charlotte with some suggestions on how the manuscript could be improved. He certainly loved it and wanted it to be as good as it possibly could be. Charlotte responded to Smith Elder & Co. on 12 September 1847 with the reply that many, if not most, writers dream of sending:

> I have received your letter and thank you for the judicious remarks and sound advice it contains. I am however not in a position to follow the advice; my engagements will not permit me to revise "Jane Eyre" a third time, and perhaps there is little to regret in the circumstance; you probably know from personal experience that an author never writes well until he has got the full spirit of his work, and were I to retrench, to alter and to add now when I am uninterested and cold, I know I should only further injure what may already be defective.[126]

William would write and receive from Charlotte, over the next four years, around two hundred letters. Theirs was a regular and often frequent correspondence. That only one of William's letters has survived is a tragedy. However, in Charlottes letters, it is possible to draw strong inferences about him, his thinking and his family. These letters were kept carefully by William and then their custody was taken over by his son Thornton who lent them to Clement Shorter as source material for his book *Charlotte Brontë and Her Circle*.[127] The letters, many of which were reproduced in full by Shorter, facilitate something of a narrative thread that spans most of Charlotte's short writing career. The letters are, in many places, quite beautiful.[128] They are full of interest, nuance and relevance and so I quote many of them - particularly those of 1848 which shed light on William - in full or nearly so.

William begins the process of guiding his new author, for the next letter on 24 September is about punctuation. Charlotte admits that it is not a strength of hers and so expresses gratitude at the corrections made. In less than a month, on 19 October 1847, six printed copies of *Jane Eyre* arrive at Haworth and Charlotte expresses to the firm her delight at the 'good paper, clear type and seemly outside'.

A letter held in the Brontë Parsonage sheds light on William as a future mentor and Charlotte as inexperienced novelist:

W.S. Williams

October 4th, 1847

Dear Sir,

I thank you sincerely for your last letter; it is valuable to me because it furnishes me with a sound opinion on points respecting which I desire to be advised: be assured I shall do what I can to profit by your wise and good counsel.

Permit me however, Sir, to caution you against forming too favourable an idea of my powers or too sanguine an appreciation of what they can achieve. I am, myself, sensible both of deficiencies of capacity and disadvantages of circumstance which will, I fear, render it somewhat difficult for me to attain popularity as an author. The eminent writers you mention – Mr Thackeray, Mr Dickens, Mrs Marsh &c., doubtless enjoyed facilities for observation such as I have not; certainly they possess a knowledge of the world, whether intuitive or acquired, such as I can lay no claim to – and this gives their writings an importance and a variety greatly beyond what I can offer the public.

Still – if health be spared and time vouchsafe to me, I mean to do my best, and should a moderate success crown my efforts, its value will be greatly enhanced by the proof it will seem to give that your kind counsel and encouragement have not been bestowed on one.[129]

The remainder of the letter has been lost. However, I can surely imagine William gathering in his mind a selection of books for Charlotte to read to expand her horizons.

Critical comment seems to have followed quickly, as Charlotte's letter of 28 October (now personally to William but still under the signature of Currer Bell) makes clear as she thanks him for writing. The world of literary criticism was one William knew well. He knew the editors and reviewers of those companies for which he had worked, but also other periodicals such as *The Weekly Chronicle* and *Quarterly Review*. He took 'meticulous care' in choosing which reviews to send to Charlotte.[130]

The review in *The Athenaeum* appeared in the edition of 23 October 1847 and, in the annotated copy, it is attributed to Chorley.[131] It is short, as befits a first novel, and comes in the section, 'Our Literary Table'. Chorley writes not in terms of Jane Eyre being radical, but rather as a very good story. 'There is so much power in this novel as to make us overlook certain eccentricities in the event invention, which trench in one or two places on what is improbable, if not unpleasant.' He then summarises the story, not omitting mildly critical comment on the melodrama of the ending, before concluding: 'As exciting strong interest of its old fashioned kind, "Jane Eyre" deserves high praise, and commendation to the novel-reader who prefers story to philosophy, pedantry, or Puseyite controversy'.

William also knew other authors, ones whose views counted. Top amongst these was WM Thackeray. William Makepeace Thackeray was born in India in 1811. His funeral, following his death in 1863, is described in a later chapter. Perhaps his best-known work, *Vanity Fair*, had been published in *Punch* in nineteen instalments from 1847 to 1848 and then as a single volume in 1848 by Bradbury and Evans with the subtitle 'A Novel without a Hero'. As Cannadine points out, Thackeray, too, was a radical writer who was quite happy to take well-deserved swipes at the ruling classes. *Jane Eyre,* though, did not do that. It is clear from Charlotte's letter that William had forwarded favourable comment by Thackeray, which delighted Charlotte and prompted a, perhaps, characteristic comment: 'I feel honoured in being approved by Mr Thackeray because I approve Mr Thackeray'. She then back-peddles a little by adding, 'This may sound presumptuous perhaps, but I mean that I have long recognised in his writing genuine talent such as I admired, such as I wondered at and delighted in'.[132] It is unlikely that the kindly William would have put her down. Indeed, we can infer that he, too, delighted in the positive critical acclaim from Thackeray and the periodicals. Thackeray had written to William on 23 October saying:

> My dear Sir, I wish you had not sent me Jane Eyre. It interested me so much that I have lost (or won if you like) a whole day in reading it at the busiest period, with the printers I know waiting for copy. Who the author can be I can't guess - if a woman she knows her language better than most ladies do or has the classical education. It is a fine book though - the man and woman capital - the style very generous and upright so to speak. I thought it was Kinglake for some time. The plot of the story is one with which I am familiar. Some of the love passages made me cry - to the astonishment of John who came in with the coals - St John the missionary is a failure I think but a good failure; there are parts excellent. I don't know why I tell you this but that I have been exceedingly moved and pleased by Jane Eyre. It is a woman's writing but whose? Give my respect and thanks to the author - whose novel is the first English one (and the French are only romances now) that I have been able to read for many a day. Yours very truly my dear Sir, WM Thackeray.[133]

Years later, he recalled the incident in his memoirs:

One day I was working frantically on a number of Vanity Fair; the manuscript of a new novel was sent round to me by William Williams literary assistant in the firm of Smith Elder & Co. I groaned at the sight of it - there was positively no time to read other people's work when I have my own to write. But I took it up, out of curiosity, resolved only to read a page or two. Before I knew what was happening, I was entirely lost. The novel was Jane Eyre by someone calling themselves Currer Bell. I say calling themselves, for I was convinced the author was a woman[...]I believe my praise helped to get the book published.[134]

Some time later, it seems clear that either Charlotte had herself responded to Mr Thackeray or more probably that William had passed on her comments, for he received this reply:

My dear Mr Williams,

I am quite vexed that by some blundering of mine I should have delayed answering Currer Bell's enormous compliment so long. I didn't know what to say in reply: it quite flustered and upset me - Is it true I wonder? &c - but a truce to egotism - thank you for your kindness in sending me the volumes, and (indirectly) for the greatest compliment I have ever received in my life.

Yours faithfully

WM Thackeray[135]

When I read this exchange with Thackeray, I feel sure that I see two men who already know each other. This contrasts with George Smith's comment, referred to in *The House of Smith Elder,* that, in order for Charlotte to meet

Thackeray, William 'boldly called upon him and asked him to dinner'.[136] Huxley recalls George Smith saying that he had asked William if he knew Thackeray and William reported that they had a slight acquaintance. On the strength of this William had been despatched to see if Smith Elder & Co. could publish *Vanity Fair*. Some years later, Smith and Thackeray were talking; it seems that Thackeray had forgotten the visit as he says, "My good friend you should have come yourself". Well, who knows?

Charlotte's relationship with Thackeray offers a fascinating insight into this woman of raw talent. He was, by a long way, the person whom she most wanted to impress. She later met him and wrote to her father on 5 December 1849 to tell of her impression. She ends by saying that 'It is better - I should think to have him as a friend than an enemy - for he is a most formidable looking personage'.[137]

Back in 1847, the gender and identity of Currer Bell would remain a mystery for a good while longer although William and George Smith already had their suspicions.

William had many friends and acquaintances among writers. One was, of course, his neighbour George Henry Lewes. William obviously had sent Lewes a copy of *Jane Eyre*, for Charlotte wrote to him on 6 November 1847 responding to his friendly criticism of the need to beware of Melodrame and the need to adhere to the principles he advocated that she 'determined to take Nature and Truth as my sole guides and to follow in their very footprints; I restrained imagination, eschewed romance, repressed excitement: over-bright colouring I avoided, and sought to produce something which should be soft, grave and true'.[138]

Lewes's public views on *Jane Eyre* would be published in *Fraser's Magazine* and Charlotte awaited these with a degree of trepidation. She wrote to William expressing her anxiety in typically stoical terms. 'I can await his critical sentence with fortitude: even if it goes against me, I shall not murmur; ability and honesty have right to condemn where they think condemnations is deserved'.[139]

William was exercising great care in feeding views on *Jane Eyre* through to Charlotte. He must have been relieved, but also pleased, that both Thackeray and Lewes had been so positive. The same was not to be the case when Charlotte read Lewes's review of her next book, *Shirley*. Charlotte had, in her contract with Smith Elder & Co., agreed to write two further books and it is clear that William had explored the options with Charlotte. Her reply of 14 December 1847 might well have left him feeling somewhat frustrated. 'I think it would be premature in me to undertake a serial now; I am not yet qualified for the task: I have neither gained sufficient firm footing with the public, nor do I possess sufficient confidence in myself, nor can I boast those unflagging animal spirits, that even command of the faculty of composition, which, as you say and I am persuaded, most justly, is an indispensable requisite to success in serial literature'.[140]

Jane Eyre was enjoying much public acclaim and William wrote to Charotte seeking a preface to a second edition. In her reply she is at pains to tell William of the great pleasure his letters bring to her: 'they seem to introduce such light and life to the torpid retirement where we lie like dormice'. William would have had to have been very thick-skinned not to feel a sense of elation.

Charlotte and her sisters, Anne and Emily, and their brother Branwell, had been writing in their lonely Yorkshire parsonage all through their childhood. The three Brontë sisters had taken the nom de plume of Bell with first names of Ellis for Emily, Acton for Anne and, of course, Currer for Charlotte. In her letter to William of 6 November 1847 Charlotte tells him that 'a prose work by Ellis and Acton Bell will soon appear.[141]' The prose works were *Wuthering Heights* and *Agnes Grey*. Newby had agreed to publish the first two, but only if the authors contributed to the cost. Charlotte had pressed on to find a publisher who would actually pay her, as she was determined to earn her living as a writer. She had sent it to a good number, only to receive it back, time and again, with notes of rejection.[142] She had of course succeeded with Smith, Elder & Co. Charlotte's concern, now expressed to William, was the time it was taking for her sisters' publisher, Mr Newby, to get their books into print. William had written to Charlotte words of strong encouragement on reading *Wuthering Heights* and *Agnes Grey*. Charlotte responded by expressing her low opinion of their publisher, Mr Newby.[143] The books were finally published in December 1847.

22 December 1847 was the day set for the meeting of the Society of Arts to which William would present his paper *On Lithography*. The paper ran to some ten thousand words and encapsulated some seventeen years of his work at Hullmandel and, of course, his writings on art for *The Athenaeum, Spectator* and others. It was William the art writer. More than that, it was William back to very near his roots. The Society of Arts had moved into the House within the Adelphi between the Strand and the River Thames in the mid eighteenth century. The Adelphi, and so the House, had been remarkable classical style buildings bearing the indelible mark of Adam, their architect. As a boy, it is surely likely that William would have ventured over the Strand to marvel at Adam's creation.

Now, nearing fifty, William was to address the Society. He had worked on his paper with the revered Henry Cole and so the atmosphere would have been heavy with expectation. Surely William, for all his reserved manner, would have been excited. We can imagine him climbing the stairs, certainly shy, but surely elated. The paper must have taken a good while to deliver. For its reception I turn to the newspaper reports of the time.

The Morning Post of Thursday 23 December said that 'Mr Williams was very warmly applauded frequently throughout his reading of the communication. The walls of the room were thickly hung with most beautiful specimens of lithography'. Bell's Weekly Messenger for Monday 27 December added:

> The different modes of lithography [...]were successfully illustrated in a clear amusing manner. The lecture was rendered the more interesting from the abundance of very beautiful illustrations which, through the kindness of several gentlemen, had been supplied for the purpose. After the meeting several members set on foot a lithographic club, a society which will devote its labours to the production of "gems" that branch of art.

The very positive reception of the paper must, I'm sure, have inspired William to write more on the subject, which, as we will see, he did. I have to say that I would have loved to have been a fly on the wall after the presentation, as the shy William mingled with his audience. The paper itself was a tour de force, but this was also the man who had discovered the mysterious Currer Bell and what was, certainly to establishment figures, a truly shocking novel but to the liberal intelligentsia something quite revolutionary - a breath of fresh air.

Leonard Huxley writes that 'among the Smith-Elder papers are preserved reviews of the *Critic, Tablet, New Monthly Magazine, Morning Post, Sun, Spectator, People's Journal and British Quarterly*[...]everybody has been praising *Jane Eyre* and for once everybody has been right'.[144]

There was most defi*nitely another school of thought, as highlighted by Rebecca Fraser. She directs attention to The Sunday Times* and *Mirror* who were concerned that Bell 'was never content until he had passed the outworks of conventional reserve'. This, she said, 'epitomises the revolutionary and dangerous disregard of custom which was the hallmark of Currer Bell'.[145]

Such was, and is the lot of the author, that the final letter of 1847 showed how hurt and angered Charlotte had been when she read a review of *Jane Eyre* in the *Spectator* which spoke of 'trickery' and 'artifice'. William surely would have had in his mind his editor's mantra: 'The *Spectator* is not enthusiastic and must not be'.

William replied quickly, for, on 4 January 1848, we begin to see the role he would take as Charlotte's guide and comforter, as she writes:

> It would take a great deal to crush me, because I know, in the first place, that my own intentions were correct; that I feel in my heart a deep reverence for Religion, that impiety is very abhorrent to me; and in the second, I place firm reliance on the judgement of some who have encouraged me. You and Mr Lewes are quite as good authorities in my estimation as Mr Dilke or the editor of the Spectator, and I would not under any circumstances, or for opprobrium regard with shame what my friends had approved: none but a coward would let the detraction of an enemy outweigh the encouragement of a friend. You must not therefore fulfil your threat of being less communicative in future; you must kindly tell me all'.[146]

William found it hard to honour this request, as we shall see in relation to the reviews of her last novel, *Villette*, perhaps being more inclined to kindness than frankness. This letter also tells us that William had shared with Charlotte the views on *Jane Eyre* of Leigh Hunt but also Julia Kavanagh. George Lewes's review appeared in *Fraser's Magazine* and Charlotte wrote to Lewes on 12 January with heartfelt thanks. Lewes clearly had encouraged Charlotte to read more widely for she admits that she has got hold of *Pride and Prejudice* and 'studied it'. The views she expresses on Miss Austen's work are typically forthright. 'An accurate daguerreotyped portrait of a common-place face; a carefully fenced, highly cultivated garden with neat borders and delicate flowers -

but no glance of a bright vivid physiognomy - no open country - no fresh air - no blue hill - no bonny beck'.[147]

The broader focus of William's and indeed Charlotte's worlds is perhaps evidenced by her letters to him of 13 and 22 January 1848. Her concern is Julia Kavanagh, who had, by then, moved on from Campden Hill Terrace and correspondence suggests that she and her mother were staying at 7 Allison Terrace, Church Street, Kensington. This is some of what Charlotte says:

> I was much interested in your account of Miss Kavanagh; the character you sketch belongs to a class I peculiarly esteem: one in which the endurance combines with exertion, talent with goodness: where genius is found only marred by extravagance, self-reliance unalloyed by self complacency. It is a character which is I believe rarely found except where there has been toil to undergo and adversity to struggle against: it will only grow to perfection in poor soil and in the shade: if the soil be too indigent, the shade too dank and thick, of course it dies where it had sprung; but I trust this will not be the case with Miss Kavanagh; I trust she will struggle erelong into the sunshine. In you she has a kind friend to direct her and I hope mother will live to see the daughter who yields to her such childlike duty, both happy and successful.[148]

Julia Kavanagh's character, her relationship with both William and his wife, and their shared concern for humanity is further underscored by a letter that Julia Kavanagh sent to Margaret Williams on 13 March 1850, pleading the case for Roman refugees:

> My dear Mrs Williams,
>
> I know your kind heart and liberal feeling. I know also that you are so happy to possess liberal and

influential friends, and I believe the case I wish to lay before you is fully worthy of their compassion and respect.

I allude to the Roman refugees, about fifty of whom are now in London and have been for some time dependent for their daily bread on the funds placed by public liberality at the disposal of the committee chosen for that purpose.

Funds are now exhausted and next week the unhappy men will be left destitute. Some have been badly wounded; others are in ill-health; very few can work or even procure work; banished from Italy, shut out from France, England is their forced place of refuge and here nothing awaits them but starvation.

Is not this a case for an appeal to the generous and liberal feelings now so active and universal? Those who for the sake of principle, a sacred sight, forget selfish wisdom and themselves by a resistance to oppression, unavailing resistance perhaps but surely most heroic, deserve something beyond mere sympathy.

When a friend of mine - as powerless as myself - mentioned these facts to me I immediately thought of Dr Epps. I thought that his high character and standing; that his well-known liberality and love of freedom entitled him to interfere in a matter in which I felt very well that insignificant individuals like myself had no right to meddle; for this I need scarcely say is no case for mere individual charity.

It may be that Doctor Epps already knows of the distress which threatens those unhappy refugees; but if he should not some good and no harm can come from mentioning the matter to him. As you are so happy as to know him you will perhaps do so! I feel at least that I can leave this case to your good judgement and kind heart, and I am too well acquainted with the latter to apologise for troubling you on such a subject.

Yours truly Julia Kavanagh[149]

Eileen Fauset tells, in her introduction to her wonderful book on Kavanagh, that Julia suffered from a curvature of the spine. Dr George Napoleon Epps made this condition his speciality and so it is entirely possible that whilst Julia was living with the Williamses she met him. The Epps were clearly friends with the Williams, Dr Epps's daughter Emily would marry William's son Robert. Fauset goes on to say that Julia's father, Morgan, was living at 28 Dean Street and that two of his sub-tenants were Karl Marx and his wife. It has to remain a matter of speculation as to whether William ever met them.

William's life included regular trips to the theatre. In her book *The Art of Adapting Victorian Literature, 1848-1920 Dramatizing Jane Eyre*, Karen Laird describes William as an 'experienced theatre critic.' She goes on to say that he had seen a dramatization of *Jane Eyre* at London's 'raucous Victoria Theatre'. [150] The vivid description that William provided prompted from Charlotte in her letter of 15 February 1848 these words, 'you have raised the veil from a corner of your great world - your London - and have shown me a glimpse of what I might call loathsome, but which I prefer to call strange.[151]' Sadly, William's description had been lost.

It is clear from Charlotte's letters that she did not favour dramatization. William is also faced with an author doubting her ability to produce the second novel required under her contract and I see in his actions that he begins to make a gentle effort at broadening her mind. Margaret Smith shares this view and expands on it in her paper for *Brontë Studies* entitled 'A Window on the World: Charlotte

Brontë's Correspondence with Her Publishers' to which I refer in more detail in chapter 7. [152]

6 BRONTË YEARS - FRIENDSHIP

We now come to the stage in Charlotte's correspondence when she begins to write to William more as a friend. As I tell later, Elizabeth Gaskell wrote this of Charlotte's letters to William: 'I like the series of letters which you sent better than any other, excepting one but I have seen'. Clement Shorter, who published *Charlotte Brontë and Her Circle* in the 1890s using mainly her letters, has this to say:

> The letters to Mr Williams are far and away the best that Charlotte wrote, at least of those which have been preserved. They are full of literary enthusiasm and of intellectual interest [...] They are an honour both to writer and receiver, and, in fact, reflect the mind of the one as much as the mind of the other.[153]

I want to pause before diving again into the letters themselves, because it seems right to step back and take a look at William. Barely three years earlier he had been utterly fed up. He had moved jobs and, just as he had settled, he hit upon gold dust - one of the greatest nineteenth century novelists - and her first published book had taken the world by storm. Had they known who she was, she would have been a celebrity. I suspect that William's reputation was also riding high. And that all before the Society of Arts meeting where he had been highly acclaimed; people had laughed at his wit and admired his craft. At the age of forty-eight he must have felt in his prime. I can't help thinking that, buoyed up by this, he takes pen and paper and writes to his newest author about a subject, for him, of all-consuming interest.

Charlotte's letter of 25 February 1848 is, thus, all about French politics and the revolutionary rising in Paris, which had begun with rioting on 22 February and ended with the abdication of Louis Philippe on 24 February and the proclamation of the Second Republic the following day.[154] Reading the letter it is possible to infer William's thoughts on the subject:

> My dear Sir, — I thank you for your note; its contents moved me much, though not to unmingled feelings of exultation. Louis Philippe (unhappy and sordid old man!) and M. Guizot doubtless merit the sharp lessons they are now being taught, because they have both proved themselves men of dishonest hearts. And every struggle any nation makes in the cause of Freedom and Truth has something noble in it — something that makes me wish it success; but I cannot believe that France — or at least Paris — will ever be the battle-ground of true Liberty, or the scene of its real triumphs. I fear she does not know "how genuine glory is put on". Is that strength to be found in her which will not bend "but in magnanimous meekness"? Have not her "unceasing changes" as yet always brought "perpetual emptiness"? Has Paris the materials within her for thorough reform? Mean, dishonest Guizot being discarded, will any better successor

be found for him than brilliant, un-principled Thiers?

But I damp your enthusiasm, which I would not wish to do, for true enthusiasm is a fine feeling whose flash I admire wherever I see it.[155]

The French Revolution of 1789 had turned upside down much of accepted notions of government and authority. The Napoleonic Wars that followed had been injurious, but ultimately had resulted in victory for the British in the person of Charlotte's hero, the Duke of Wellington. William was much more on the side of the Revolution and the movements that it sparked in Britain. The Reform Act had failed to extend the franchise to him. The Corn Laws had led to much suffering as a result of high food prices. The Chartist movement, with its aim of extending the franchise, had run out of steam, so to have a fresh revolution on the other side of the Channel would have been music to his ears.

William's circle (of George Lewes and Leigh Hunt but also Thomas Carlyle) was always likely to be sympathetic to those standing against authority. I wonder whether William's own sympathies could be traced back to the long experience of his own family in Wheatley and its place in the English Civil War. There was also the 'family myth' that the Williamses were descended from Oliver Cromwell. Certainly those in his circle would all have read Carlyle's account of the Revolution of 1789. They would know his work on Chartism and his piece, *Past and Present,* on the darker side of industrialisation.

William might also have benefitted from his brother in law's first hand view of France that year. There is in the family archive, a letter from Robert Hill writing from St Pol de Léon in Brittany to his sister Sophia. It is about family matters but it does end with 'little Charley' joining Robert and his sister Emily in sending love. Little Charley, then aged six, was the son of William's lifelong friend

Charles Wells.

The February Revolution was also the subject of Charlotte's letter of 28 February. William had sent he a copy of *The Examiner* from 26 February, which was dominated by events in France. By 1848, *The Examiner* was being edited by John Forster, but it continued its mission of independence with which it had been founded by Leigh Hunt and his brother. This is how the edition of 26 February began:

> Another revolution has been accomplished in Paris and Louis Philippe is no longer King of the French. He has been deposed and cast out from the throne which he promised eighteen years ago to surround with Republican institutions and which he laboured ever since to make to despotic and absolute. There is therefore not one group or class of intelligent men in Europe that will not have received with some pleasure in the midst of all the anxiety created, intelligence of the signal discomfiture of all the scheming, building, bribing, tyrannising, and diplomatising of Louis Philippe.

A brief survey of the other weekly editions for 1848 reveals that this revolution was very much to the fore. Margaret Smith is very clear of William's views on the revolutions, 'He was one of the London republicans'.[156] Charlotte wrote again a few days later, commenting on the newspaper reports and making this intriguing observation:

> How strange it appears to see literary and scientific names figuring in the list of members of a Provisional Government! How would it sound if Carlyle and Sir John Herschel and Tennyson and Mr. Thackeray and Douglas Jerrold were selected to manufacture a new constitution for England? Whether do such men sway the public

mind most effectually from their quiet studies or from a council-chamber?[157]

Smith Elder & Co were very close to publishing a major work on probably the 'greatest political mind in the French Assembly', Honoré Gabriel Riqueti, Comte de Mirabeau, who had risen to prominence following the Revolution of 1789.[158] This emerges from Charlotte's letter to William of 15 June where she thanks him for sending the piece on Mirabeau and asks whether the author is a 'Manchester man', noting a 'savour of Carlyle's peculiarities of style'. In her note, Margaret Smith provides an answer in the affirmative, adding his name - John Stores Smith - and his profession - Managing Director of the Sheepbridge Iron and Coal Company near Chesterfield in Derbyshire.

William soon guides the correspondence back to Charlotte's own publications when he suggests that she should consider illustrating *Jane Eyre*. From William, having spent years with Hullmandel, this was natural enough. It, perhaps, was also natural enough, given Charlotte's heroine's fondness and ability for drawing. Thackeray was illustrating *Vanity Fair* to great effect. In her reply of 11 March, Charlotte found herself forced to admit that she lacked the necessary skill and so had to decline. All the time, for all William's kindness, he was seeking ways to achieve further commercial success for Charlotte and his own firm.

Looking at the permanent exhibition at the Brontë Parsonage, it is education that shouts loudest. Patrick Brontë was determined that his son and daughters should be well versed in literature, painting and politics. There are examples of Charlotte's painting - copies of illustrations in a book by Byron - clear evidence of her ability, although the exhibition points out that her skill was in copying; it was Branwell who could 'paint from nature'. Long, dark winter evenings gave abundant scope for study and practice. Notwithstanding this, Charlotte remained firm in her refusal to illustrate her work.

Part of William's plan for Charlotte was to introduce her to a wider range of reading. He sends her G.H. Lewes's most recent novel, *Rose, Blanche and Violet*, seeking her views before he offers his own. She responds in detail on 26 April. William then sends his critique, to which Charlotte responds at length on 1 May. Reading the letters, it seems to me that William has begun to assume the mantle of literary tutor, encouraging his pupil to delve into the detail of what Lewes has written and how he has written it. Another piece by Lewes that Charlotte studied was his play *The Noble Heart*. With this, she was more forthright in her views of its shortcomings, as she writes in her letter of 22 February 1850 "It was cheering and pleasant to read it for, in your animated description, I seemed to realise the scene. Lewes is a strange being [. . .] he seems to me clever, sharp and coarse [. . .] Nothing truly great, I should think, will he ever produce. Yet he merits just such successes as the one you describe - triumphs public, brief and noisy - Notoriety suits Lewes".[159]

Charlotte's next letter of 12 May is quite different in that now she becomes the tutor and William the pupil. William has asked her views on the career of a governess, quite probably taking a cue from the story of *Jane Eyre*, and she takes a large piece of paper and writes at length on a subject that would recur in their correspondence and that was clearly of the utmost importance to William: education and most particularly his daughters' education. Before looking at the letter, may I pause for William is still, at this stage, writing to Currer Bell. He may have his suspicions as to the gender of his correspondent, but he has not yet met Charlotte.

> Some remarks in your last letter on teaching commanded my attention. I suppose you never were engaged in tuition yourself; but if you had been, you could not have more exactly hit on the great qualification — I had almost said the one

great qualification — necessary to the task: the faculty, not merely of acquiring but of imparting knowledge — the power of influencing young minds — that natural fondness for, that innate sympathy with, children, which, you say, Mrs. Williams is so happy as to possess. He or she who possesses this faculty, this sympathy — though perhaps not otherwise highly accomplished — need never fear failure in the career of instruction. Children will be docile with them, will improve under them; parents will consequently repose in them confidence. Their task will be comparatively light, their path comparatively smooth. If the faculty be absent, the life of a teacher will be a struggle from beginning to end. No matter how amiable the disposition, how strong the sense of duty, how active the desire to please; no matter how brilliant and varied the accomplishments; if the governess has not the power to win her young charge, the secret to instil gently and surely her own knowledge into the growing mind entrusted to her, she will have a wearing, wasting existence of it. To educate a child, as I daresay Mrs. Williams has educated her children, probably with as much pleasure to herself as profit to them, will indeed be impossible to the teacher who lacks this qualification.

Norman Penty suggests that William indeed might have had some experience of teaching at Clarke's school before starting his apprenticeship. Charlotte continues:

But, I conceive, should circumstances — as in the case of your daughters — compel a young girl notwithstanding to adopt a governess's profession, she may contrive to instruct and even to instruct well. That is, though she cannot form the child's mind, mould its character, influence its dis-position, and guide its conduct as she would wish, she may give lessons — even good, clear, clever lessons in the various branches of knowledge. She may earn and doubly earn her scanty salary as a daily governess. As a schoolteacher she may succeed; but as a resident governess she will never (except under peculiar and exceptional circumstances) be happy. Her deficiency will harass her not so much in school-time as in play-hours; the moments that would be rest and recreation to the governess who understood and could adapt herself to children, will be almost torture to her who has lost that power. Many a time, when her charge turns unruly on her hands, when the responsibility which she would wish to discharge faithfully and perfectly, becomes unmanageable to her, she will wish herself a housemaid or kitchen girl, rather than a baited, trampled, desolate, distracted governess.

This is about halfway through a long letter and I wonder how William felt? It seems to me that Charlotte most certainly is here assuming the mantle of William's teacher. She is surely also drawing on the character of *Jane Eyre* both as a governess and teacher. The letter continues with further thoughts of the role of governess and then this particular guidance on William's daughter Fanny:

As for that one who, you say, has a nervous horror of exhibition, I need not beg you to be gentle with her; I am sure you will not be harsh, but she must be firm with herself, or she will repent it in after life. She should begin by degrees to endeavour to overcome her diffidence. Were she destined to enjoy an independent, easy existence, she might respect her natural disposition to seek retirement, and even cherish it as a shade-loving virtue; but since that is not her lot, since she is fated to make her way in the crowd, and to depend on herself, she should say: I will try and learn the art of self-possession, not that I may display my accomplishments, but that I may have the satisfaction of feeling that I am my own mistress, and can move and speak undaunted by the fear of man. While, however, I pen this piece of advice, I confess that it is much easier to give than to follow. What the sensations of the nervous are under the gaze of publicity none but the nervous know; and how powerless reason and resolution are to control them would sound incredible except to the actual sufferers.[160]

As we shall see, William quite possibly followed this advice concerning Fanny, although, sadly, her diffidence would come to cause her grief later in her life. Charlotte ends her letter with expressions of amusement at rumours about her true identity and a postscript with thoughts about her next book.

William is not put off by anything Charlotte has written; indeed, he must have asked again when, in her letter of 2 June Charlotte comments further on his reference to his family and to his daughters. The 1851 census shows that his eldest daughter Ellen was then a 'daily governess' and that her sister Fanny Emily was a teacher of music. We can infer from Charlotte's letters to William that he was much concerned about his daughters earning their living. Charlotte writes again at great length on 15 June, commenting first upon a recent holiday that William and his family must have taken at the Hill family home in Broxbourne:

I saw the pretty south-of-England village, so different from our northern congregations of smoke-dark houses clustered round their soot-

> vomiting mills. I saw in your description, fertile, flowery Essex — a contrast indeed to the rough and rude, the mute and sombre yet well-beloved moors overspreading this corner of Yorkshire. I saw the white school-house, the venerable school-master — I even thought I saw you and your daughters; and in your second letter I see you all distinctly, for, in describing your children, you unconsciously describe yourself.
>
> I may well say that your letters are of value to me, for I seldom receive one but I find something in it which makes me reflect, and reflect on new themes. Your town life is somewhat different from any I have known, and your allusions to its advantages, troubles, pleasures, and struggles are often full of significance to me.

She then continues with clear advice on the route that young women (William's daughters) should take through life:

> I have always been accustomed to think that the necessity of earning one's subsistence is not in itself evil; but I feel it may become a heavy evil if health fails, if employment lacks, if the demand upon our efforts made by the weakness of others dependent upon us, becomes greater than our strength suffices to answer...Most desirable then it is that all - both men and women - should have the power and the will to work for themselves; most advisable that both sons and daughters should early be inured to habits of independence and industry.

She sets this into context by adding:

> It seems to me that your kind heart is pained by the thought of what your daughter may suffer if transplanted from a free and indulged home-

existence to a life of constraint and labour among strangers.

It is possible to see in Charlotte's words some of William's own thinking on the matter:

> I think you speak excellent sense when you say that girls without fortune should be brought up and accustomed to support themselves; and that if they marry poor men, it should be with a prospect of being able to help their partners. If all parents thought so, girls would not be reared on speculation with a view to making mercenary marriages - and consequently women would not be so piously degraded as they now so often are.

She goes on to say:

> You speak sense again when you express a wish that Fanny were placed in a position where active duties would engage her attention; where her faculties would be exercised and her mind occupied [...] Fanny may feel sure of this; if she intends to be an Artist's wife she had better try an apprenticeship with Fortune as a governess, first; she cannot undergo a better preparation for that honourable (honourable if rightly considered) but certainly not luxurious destiny.[161]

Margaret Smith adds that 'Fanny Williams was evidently talented. She is said to have had an even finer voice than her youngest sister Anna who made her name as soprano soloist'.[162] Her note suggests that Charlotte's broadly positive view of the profession of governess was, in time, tempered and that she 'presented a rather different view of the damaging effects of a governess' experience on the timid, long-suffering Mrs Pryor in *Shirley*'[163].

The theme of education will recur a number of times in William's story, not least in the views that Ruskin held of women's education about which he wrote in *The Ethics of the Dust* and which I explore in Chapter 11.

Three subjects come together in Charlotte's letter to William of 22 June 1848. The first concerns Mirabeau and the error she sees in his biographer being too ready to praise him. Her view of him is quite the opposite. It is interesting that in Shorter's edition, this is the totality of the letter, and it speaks clearly to the quiet efforts William is making in sharpening Charlotte's critical faculties. In Margaret Smith's edition there are two additional passages which shed further light on William. The first of these is a continuation of his concerns about his daughters' professions. The second goes to the heart of this complex man. We can infer that he has been contemplating his own career and has found it seriously wanting. As Charlotte writes, 'for thirty-five years to have filled a position where your tastes had no scope, and your facilities no exercise, is sad indeed'. She offers comfort by stressing the joys of his family but concludes that such suggestions are 'very clumsy'; his 'cup of life must often have been a bitter one'.[164] This comes barely four months after William had been riding high. He was surely a man given to depression.

Suddenly everything changes. Charlotte had been working on the manuscript of her second novel, *Shirley* and her sister had published *The Tenant of Wildfell Hall* in the name of Acton Bell. Charlotte wrote to her friend Mary Taylor:

> About two months since, I had a letter from my publishers, Smith & Elder – saying that "Jane Eyre" had had a great run in America – and that a publisher there had consequently bid high for the first sheets of the next work of "Currer Bell" which they had promised to let him have.
>
> Presently after came a second missive from Smith & Elder – all in alarm, suspicions and wrath – their American corres-pondent [sic] had written

to them complaining that the first sheets of a new work of "Currer Bell" had already been received and not by their house but by a rival publisher – and asking the meaning of such false play – it enclosed an extract from a letter from Mr Newby (A&E Bell's publisher) affirming 'that to the best of his belief "Jane Eyre"- "Wuthering Heights" – "Agnes Grey" – and the "Tenant of Wildfell Hall" (the new work) were all the production of one writer'.[165]

With this explosive news, Anne and Charlotte had no choice but to take the train to London on 7 July to go to 65 Cornhill and admit all to Charlotte's publisher.

May I break the narrative one more time to digress on the word 'train'? Of all the revolutions going on around William, that of the rapid and massive introduction of the railway was probably the greatest. A decade or so earlier, a trip to London from Yorkshire would have been both long and uncomfortable - a trip of perhaps three days. Jane Eyre took a day to cover the fifty miles back to Thornfield. Eric Hobsbawm, in his book *The Age of Revolution*, highlights the development of railways as 'dramatic, surprising and fortuitous'.[166] The early nineteenth century witnessed the amassing of even greater wealth by the few - mainly landowners but also those brave enough to dive into the hothouse of industrialisation, for example, in the Lancashire cotton trade. Amassed wealth needed a home and, whilst railways actually produced only very modest returns and indeed, in some cases, large losses, they were seen as a good home for money. This resulted in the building of a remarkable network of railways that transformed the way society functioned. The frequent meeting of people living far apart became possible. Charlotte and Anne could 'pop on the train to London' and they took the night train to London on Friday 7 and Saturday 8 July. Charlotte later invested in a railway company following the advice of George Smith.

Before turning to the description of the visit (as recorded in Charlotte's letter to Mary Taylor of 4 September 1848), in order to underline its significance, I would like to quote from a paper that was delivered in a collection of essays published by the Brontë Society on the hundredth anniversary of the publication of Jane Eyre. Helen Arnold wrote:

> Had there not been the publishers' tangle in which two American firms each claimed the right to this successful new author's next book, we might never have been given that picture – so dear to all lovers of the Brontës – that of two shy Yorkshire girls standing, on the morning of July 8th, 1848, in the doorway of Mr Smith's office at 65 Cornhill. When the young publishers saw his own letter in Charlotte's hand and asked her, "Where did you get this?" one likes to remember – and we have it in her own words –that Charlotte laughed.[167]

So, to Charlotte's description:

> We found 65 - to be a large bookseller's shop in a street almost as bustling as the Strand - we went in - walked up to the counter - there were a great many young men and lads here and there - I said to the first I could accost - "May I see Mr Smith?" He hesitated, looked a little surprised - but went to fetch him - We sat down and waited awhile - looking at some books on the counter - publications of theirs well known to us - of many of which they had sent to us copies as presents. At last someone came up and said dubiously.
>
> "Did you wish to see me, Ma'am?"
>
> "Is it Mr Smith?" I said looking up through my spectacles at a young, tall gentleman.

"It is."

I then put his own letter into his hand directed to "Currer Bell". He looked at it and then at me - again - yet again - I laughed at his queer perplexity - A recognition took place. I gave my real name - "Miss Brontë". We were both hurried from the shop into a little back room - veiled with a great skylight and only large enough to hold three chairs and a desk - and there explanations were rapidly gone into ....Mr Smith hurried out and returned with one whom he introduced as Mr Williams - a pale stooping man of fifty very much like a faded Tom Dixon'.[168]

There then followed conversation, with George Smith enthusiastically suggesting all manner of introductions for Charlotte, much to her horror. She notes to Mary Taylor that Mr Williams 'understood me directly'. Charlotte's own letter to William perhaps underlines this:

TO W. S. WILLIAMS

Chapter Coffee-House, Ivy Lane,

8th July 1848

My dear Sir, — Your invitation is too welcome not to be at once accepted. I should much like to see Mrs. Williams and her children, and very much like to have a quiet chat with yourself. Would it suit you if we came to-morrow, after dinner — say about seven o'clock, and spent Sunday evening with you?

We shall be truly glad to see you whenever it is convenient to you to call. — I am, my dear sir, yours faithfully,

C. Brontë.[169]

Charlotte's letter to her friend described a number of visits, including this one, which gives us really our first picture of this intriguing man:

> Mr Williams came early to take us to church - he was so quiet but so sincere in his attentions - one could not but have a most friendly leaning toward him - he has a nervous hesitation in speech and a difficulty in finding appropriate language in which to express himself - which throws him into the background in conversation - but I have been his correspondent - and therefore knew with what intelligence he could write - so that I was no longer underrating him [...] Mr Smith is a practical man - I wish Mr Williams were more so - but he is altogether of the contemplative theorising order - Mr Williams lives too much on abstractions'.
>
> [We] then went home with Mr Williams to tea - and saw his comparatively humble but neat residence and his fine family of eight children - his wife was ill. A daughter of Leigh Hunt was there - she sung some little Italian airs which she had picked up amongst the peasantry in Tuscany'.

Many years later Anna Williams offered a recollection of that visit by Charlotte. I say a recollection, since Anna was then only three years old. It may be fair to assume that the visit had entered into the family compendium of stories, not least that, in Charlotte's account, Mrs Williams had been ill:

> One day Mr Williams told his wife that he had distant cousins coming to visit him, and he brought them to the house and introduced them under an assumed name. Mrs Smith Williams was as shrewdly practical as her husband was visionary and romantic; and, being a woman, was

not easily deceived. When those quiet, unassuming north country women were gone, she said to her husband, "unless I am much mistaken those are the Miss Brontës; in that case they must indeed be very distant cousins!" And her husband only laughed.[170]

Charlotte wrote a letter of thanks to William on 13 July:

TO W. S. WILLIAMS

Haworth, July 13th, 1848.

My dear Sir, — We reached home safely yesterday, and in a day or two I doubt not we shall get the better of the fatigues of our journey.

It was a somewhat hasty step to hurry up to town as we did, but I do not regret having taken it. In the first place, mystery is irksome, and I was glad to shake it off with you and Mr. Smith, and to show myself to you for what I am, neither more, nor less — thus removing any false expectations that may have arisen under the idea that Currer Bell had a just claim to the masculine cognomen he, perhaps somewhat presumptuously, adopted — that he was, in short, of the nobler sex.

I was glad also to see you and Mr. Smith, and am very happy now to have such pleasant recollections of you both, and of your respective families. My satisfaction would have been complete could I have seen Mrs. Williams. The appearance of your children tallied on the whole accurately with the description you had given of them. Fanny was the one I saw least distinctly; I tried to get a clear view of her countenance, but her position in the room did not favour my efforts.[171]

The meeting of William and Charlotte undoubtedly cemented their friendship, for William was then to begin what would be a long conversation about painting - something that was so very close to his heart.

7 BRONTË YEARS - ART

The more I delved into the life of this 'faded Tom Dixon', the more convinced I became that William was not only caring and intelligent, but also passionate and more than prepared to stand his corner. He loved and cared about writing, about politics, about his wife and children, about young artists and writers, but, most of all, he was passionate about art. William had sent Charlotte a copy of an article he had written for the *John Bull* magazine. She replies with quite obvious delight:

> I had just read your article in the John Bull magazine; it very clearly and fully explains the cause of the difference obvious between ancient and modern paintings. I wish you had been with us when we went over to the Exhibition and the National Gallery; a little explanation from a judge of art would doubtless have enabled us to understand better what we saw; perhaps one day, we may have this pleasure.
>
> Accept my own thanks and my sister's for your kind attention to us while in town, and — Believe me, yours sincerely,

Charlotte Brontë.[172]

The article was inspired by the Royal Academy Exhibition and addressed what William refers to as 'great and prevalent defects in the method of painting: flatness, hardness, chalkiness, and 'opacity' and the want of atmospheric effect in many out-door scenes'. He points to the 'solidity of clouds' and 'immobility of foliage.' He laments that colour in contemporary paintings 'degenerates into the opposite extremes of gaudiness and leaden blackness'. This, he contrasts with the work of 'Gainsborough, Cuyp, Ruysdael and Teniers' whose pictures have a 'luminous brilliancy…not attained by any exhibitor at the Royal Academy; to say nothing of tone'. Later in the article, William takes time and care to examine the 'peculiarities of execution' of the paintings by contemporary British artists exhibited in the then Royal Academy Exhibition. He goes on to provide what strikes me as a fascinating explanation of the depiction of light in great paintings:

> We view all objects through a subtle fluid of the atmosphere and in proportion to the density of this medium and the degree in which it is illumined, we see objects more or less distinctly. Light falling on any object is reflected by it so strongly that the point nearest to the light, that at this point the light almost destroys the actual colour of the object; which only shows its proper hue at a little distance from this point of light, while those parts of the object which recede from the light, appear less vivid in colour, until their hues are altogether lost in deep shade. It is obvious, therefore, that at every degree of remoteness from the light (as it appears to the spectator) the colour of the object undergoes modification.

The article continues with equally careful analysis of the process of painting:

> Thus, then, the painter has to represent with pigments on plane surface, the luminous quality of light and the transparent depth of shade, as well as the intervening gradations of hue and texture. And his picture also is influenced by the light that falls upon it, the qualities of the pigments [...] Certain colours absorb the light and others reflect it, more or less, according to their hues and density [...] Shadows painted with opaque pigments, however thinly laid on, or dark the hue, will always reflect light in some degree and therefore the transparent depth essential for deep shadow will be wanting [...] Now although many modern artists glaze freely [...] they do not exclusively employ transparent pigments for their shadows, nor do they always reserve their glazing till the last. Hence we find shadows as solid as the middle tints [...] and there seems to be no atmosphere before the objects.[173]

Margaret Smith is quite clear that, when it came down to teaching Charlotte about appreciation of art, William very much drew on his own knowledge and judgement.[174] Surely this deep understanding was earned by many hours spent at Hullmandel on lithographs and, probably more so, by studying paintings for the purpose of reviews. What strikes me as of great significance is the date of the article:

1848.

This was the Year of Revolution when also, in September, William Holman Hunt, John Everett Millais and Dante Gabriel Rossetti came together in another revolution to form the Pre Raphaelite Brotherhood born of their dissatisfaction with much of the painting that came after Raphael. Their champion was none other than John

Ruskin. William might have been unhappy that he had not achieved recognition as a writer, but, here, he is at a further point of revolution, this time in his beloved world of painting. Timothy Hilton provides a short history of how the Brotherhood came together. Dante Gabriel Rossetti was one of four children of the Italian poet Gabriele Rossetti. His siblings were William, Christina and Maria. Dante Gabriel attended the Sass's Drawing Academy and there he met Millais. He was then reluctant to attend the Royal Academy School and so he opted to become the pupil of Ford Madox Brown, firmly outside the art establishment. The two viewed the Royal Academy Exhibition of 1848 and found nothing to their taste, except one painting by Holman Hunt entitled the *The Eve of St Agnes*. The three soon discovered what they had in common and, in short, the Brotherhood was born.[175]

William's obituary in *The Publishers' Circular* wrote of his friendship with writers, but also with a great number of painters. I think there are a number of different routes through which these might have arisen. As an art critic for the important magazines of the time, he would surely have met many artists. I suspect that the relationship, which developed between William and his future son-in-law, Lowes Dickinson, was significant. Dickinson was becoming an important portrait painter with a studio in Langham Place; he was also a partner in the family printing business. The diary of Ford Madox Brown has a good number of references to him seeing Lowes Dickinson and, indeed, to Madox Brown working for him. Further reading of Madox Brown's diaries reveals more. The diaries begin at the start of 1847 when, at the age of twenty-six, Madox Brown was widowed and left with a young daughter, Lucy. These are his painter's diaries and so set out, day by day, what he does and also whom he meets. Early on in 1847, a connection is made with the Drawing Academy set up by the Dickinson brothers at 18 ½ Maddox Street. Ford visited this quite often in 1847 and 1848. In 1849, the relationship moved on, for 'he drew a figure of the Lord Jesus for the Dickinsons'.[176] He was working for them. Lowes Dickinson's letters are held by Princeton University Library and include letters from John Ruskin, Ford Madox Brown, William Holman Hunt, John Everett Millais and Dante Gabrielle Rossetti. This would point strongly to an artists' circle. William's connection with it becomes clearer later on.

Painting, and in particular Ruskin's work *Modern Painters,* was again the subject of Charlotte's letter of 31 July:

TO W.S. WILLIAMS

Haworth, July 31st, 1848.

My dear Sir, — I have lately been reading Modern Painters, and I have derived from the work much genuine pleasure and, I hope, some edification; at any rate, it made me feel how ignorant I had previously been on the subject which it treats. Hitherto I have only had instinct to guide me in judging of art; I feel more as if I had been walking blindfold — this book seems to give me eyes. I wish I had pictures within reach by which to test the new sense. Who can read these glowing descriptions of Turner's works without longing to see them? However eloquent and convincing the language in which another's opinion is placed before you, you still wish to judge for yourself. I like this author's style much: there is both energy and beauty in it; I like himself too, because he is such a hearty admirer. He does not give Turner half-measure of praise or veneration, he eulogises, he reverences him (or rather his genius) with his whole soul. One can sympathise with that sort of devout, serious admiration (for he is no rhapsodist) — one can respect it; and yet possibly many people would laugh at it.[177]

Two further articles in *Brontë Studies* expand on Charlotte and art, and so, I believe, on William's direct influence. Visual art in the writing of Charlotte Brontë is highlighted by Emily Petermann in her article on 'Lucy Snowe's Art Criticism in Villette'.[178] She shows how Snowe has a preference for simplicity. This echoes ideas explored by Charlotte and William in their correspondence and which picks up views that William expresses in his own writing on art. Jian Choe, in 'Towards Modern Aesthetics: Charlotte Brontë and J.M.W. Turner', advances arguments which draw parallels between Charlotte Brontë's descriptive writing and Turner's paintings - most particularly his watercolours.[179] Of Ruskin, Choe explains that *Modern Painters* began as an extended defence of Turner against adverse criticism in *Blackwood's* Magazine. He writes:

> Ruskin accentuates Turner's innovations and distinguishes his fidelity to nature from the idealizing traditions of landscape. He provides an in-depth analysis of the divergent ways in which Turner and contemporary topographical painters represent nature, criticizing the latter for their artificiality and inaccuracy of observation. Ruskin rightly pinpoints the light effect and the elliptical approach, which were to become central to Impressionism, as the hallmark of Turner. The critic thus appreciates his hero's rendering of 'the sparkling and evanescent light' and of 'the legitimate rain-cloud, with its ragged and spray-like edge, its veily transparency', implying that his art, in essence, involves visionary naturalism.[180]

Returning to the letter of 31 July, Charlotte continues with her admission of the pleasure she derives from William's letters. He has obviously apologised for annoying her with his views on religion and philosophy. She offers reassurance. She ends by thanking him and his family for keeping the secret of her true identity.

William has helped Charlotte to identify what might be termed the two fundamental principles she aspires to in her writing and these are the subject of her letter of 14 August. 'The first duty of an author is – I conceive – a faithful allegiance to "Truth and Nature"; his second, such a conscientious study of Art as shall enable him to interpret eloquently and effectively the oracles delivered by those two great deities'. She goes on to name Thackeray as 'the legitimate High Priest of Truth'. It is interesting that both the truth of nature and the right principles of art are at the heart of William's *John Bull* article.

Truth and nature have an echo in the writings of Ruskin. When he wrote of the Pre-Raphaelite Brotherhood, he emphasised that, when they painted a landscape, it would be a real landscape and not imagined. The people who appeared in their paintings were actual people. Kirsty Stonell Walker in her book, *Stunner*, wrote of the fall and rise of Fanny Cornforth.[181] She traces the lives of some of the women whom the members of the Brotherhood painted and we can see them placed within the London of the mid nineteenth century in the same way that we can see William and his family. It wasn't that they were wealthy women having their portraits painted; they were ordinary women placed in a picture to help tell its story. It is hard to read *Jane Eyre* without a similar sense that she is not made up; she is not a flight of fancy, but flesh and blood in the telling of a story. This is echoed in a further article from *The Brontës Then and Now*, this time by Donald Hopewell:

> A generation that revered Thackeray and worshipped Dickens was enthusiastic in its welcome of Jane and Rochester; and, as Thackeray reminded Charlotte at a later date, she achieved in a moment the success which it had taken him the work of years to accomplish [...]

The second and third volumes of the novel might be – probably were – pure creatures of the imagination, but the first volume was undoubted and obvious autobiography; only one who had suffered as Jane had done, and had watched and loved a Helen Burns in life and death could have written it; in a literary sense it had all the features of the new art of photography.[182]

William had been working on a further article on art, and, on 24 March 1849, *The Builder* magazine, with its readership of architects and designers, published this article entitled 'On the Importance of a Knowledge and Observance of the Principles of Art by Designers'. [183] Barely a month later, Charlotte concludes a letter to him by offering congratulations on the publication of John Ruskin's *The Seven Lamps of Architecture*, which, she says, 'if they resemble their predecessor, *Modern Painters*, they will be no lamps at all, but a new constellation of seven bright stars for whose rising the reading world ought to be anxiously agaze'.[184]

Taken with his paper on lithography, his reviews in *The Athenaeum* and his piece in the *John Bull* magazine on light and colour, William's article in *The Builder* adds further interest to this hitherto 'quiet grey man'. The article begins with essential principles:

> In painting, the artist has to embody his ideas of scenes, persons or incidents by a pictorial representation of natural objects; and in proportion to the skill of his design and the truth of the representation, must be the vividness with which his idea will be expressed.

Turning to how this is achieved, he says:

> It is the apparent forms, surface and hues of things that the painter has to depict, though he can only do this by understanding their real form

and nature, and the effects of light and atmosphere upon them.

He then identifies the result:

> A picture is, or should be, the representation of what is seen either in reality or in the minds eye from one point of view at one moment of time and could and should convey the impression of an idea stamped upon the mind of the painter at that moment which all fine pictures do. Design gives unity and definition to the conception.

The article goes on to explore design in practice and the types of furnishings used, patterns employed and effects created. It is a critique of the Victorian drawing room crammed with dark patterns, pictures and diverse objects, almost as if he is thinking of busy Victorian parlours such as that depicted in Holman Hunt's *Awakening Conscience* of 1853. He is, though, drawing on his views of painting before the Pre Raphaelites and he highlights errors such as painting objects in the background with the detail appropriate to those nearer to the eye of the viewer. In this regard I would expect him to approve of Turner's *Frosty Morning* of 1813 where it is hard to make out the distant carriage but where the frozen ground and labourer's tools are as clear as crystal.

I am not an artist and this is not a book about art. The point that comes through, loud and clear, from William's article is that he loves his subject and expresses clearly the views he holds. More than this though, it is an article on design and so connects with the world of Kelmscott Manor, which I mentioned in the Chapter 2, and so with Dante Gabriel Rossetti, William and Jane Morris and the Arts and Crafts movement.

Returning to William's correspondence with Charlotte, the latter part of 1848 sees a change of tone. It is foreshadowed in Charlotte's letter of 14 August, which she ends by saying, 'I hope Mrs Williams health is more satisfactory than when you last wrote'. In the years 1848 and 1849, cholera again hit London. There had been a serious outbreak in 1832, but this later one claimed some fifteen thousand lives.[185] It would, thus, not be unreasonable for William to be worried, given both the size of his family, the age of his younger children and the possibility that cholera might have taken one or both of his parents.

Whilst he seems more content with his professional lot, William is becoming increasingly anxious about his family and his continuing ability to support them. Charlotte offers words of support whilst contending with tragedy in her own life. Her brother, Branwell, dies largely from his own excesses. In her letter of 18 October 1848 there is evidence of a deepening friendship, when Charlotte offers William a little gentle criticism which opens a window onto his views of matters of religion:

> You may be sure I read your views on the providence of God and the nature of man with interest. You are already aware that in much of what you say my opinions coincide with those you express, and where they differ I shall not attempt to bias you. Thought and conscience are, or ought to be, free; and, at any rate, if your views were universally adopted there would be no persecution, no bigotry. But never try to proselytise, the world is not yet fit to receive what you and Emerson say: man, as he now is, can no more do without creeds and forms in religion than he can do without laws and rules in social inter-course. You and Emerson judge others by yourselves; all mankind are not like you, any more than every Israelite was like Nathaniel.
>
> "Is there a human being," you ask, "so depraved that an act of kindness will not touch — nay, a word melt him?" There are hundreds of human

beings who trample on acts of kindness and mock at words of affection. I know this though I have seen but little of the world. I suppose I have something harsher in my nature than you have, something which every now and then tells me dreary secrets about my race, and I cannot believe the voice of the Optimist, charm he never so wisely. On the other hand, I feel forced to listen when Thackeray speaks. I know truth is delivering her oracles by his lips.

As to the great, good, magnanimous acts which have been performed by some men, we trace them up to motives and then estimate their value; a few, perhaps, would gain and many lose by this test. The study of motives is a strange one, not to be pursued too far by one fallible human being in reference to his fellows.

Do not condemn me as uncharitable. I have no wish to urge my convictions on you, but I know that while there are many good, sincere, gentle people in the world, with whom kindness is all-powerful, there are also not a few like that false friend (I had almost written fiend) whom you so well and vividly described in one of your late letters, and who, in acting out his part of domestic traitor, must often have turned benefits into weapons wherewith to wound his benefactors. —

Believe me, yours sincerely, C. Brontë.[186]

Ralph Waldo Emerson (1803-1882), to whom Charlotte refers, is described by Lawrence Buell as the 'first public intellectual in the History of the United States.[187]' One particular connection to William was Emerson's relationship with Thomas Carlyle which, after their first meeting in 1833, was described as 'almost entirely essayistic and epistolary' and stretched over more than forty years covering a vast range of ideas and thinking. One of particular relevance to Charlotte's correspondence with William was Emerson's view of Napoleon. Buell stressed that by the mid-nineteenth century Napoleon had become a cult figure. He was the hero of the middle classes. He was the exemplification of Emerson's view of self-reliance. Charlotte had little regard for Napoleon; her hero was Wellington.

We can infer from Charlotte's letter of 5 November that William is again suffering from anxiety. It is perhaps further evidence that this is the correspondence of friends. One minute there is a conversation about the currents of religion, and the next it is all about very personal worries. Here is just a little of what she says:

> True then it is that I grieve for your sorrow and sympathise in your anxious cares: I cannot make light of them as causeless - it is evident they have a cause: you do not feel strong - you have no certainty of continued health, and yet you have a family, a large family to rear, to bring forward, to settle in life. It is easy to say - do your best and leave the rest to God; I can conceive that – try as you may to rely on Providence - the father and husband will still at times make a voice of apprehension heard in your heart.[188]

In spite of all his worries, William expresses the utmost concern for Charlotte's sister Emily, who is far from well. He suggests remedies including (eventually, but too late) the homoeopathy of his friend Dr Epps. As evidenced in a further piece by Mabel Edgerley from *The Brontës Then and Now*, Charlotte wrote on 9 December 1848 to Dr Epps, describing Emily's case: 'Her appetite failed, she evinced a constant thirst. In appearance she grew rapidly emaciated; her pulse was found to be 115 per minute. Expectoration accompanies her cough. The shortness of breath is aggravated by the slightest exertion'.[189]

As already indicated in relation to Julia Kavanagh, there were two Dr Epps whom William probably knew: Dr John Epps (1805-1869) and his half brother George Napoleon Epps (1815-1874). They were both homoeopathic practitioners. The *Dictionary of National Biography* says of John Epps that he published *Internal Evidences of Christianity Deduced from Phrenology*, that he was Medical Director of the Royal Jennerian and London Vaccine Institution, that he issued *Homoeopathy and its Principles Explained* (1841) and that he was a lecturer on Materia Medica at the Homoeopathic Hospital, Hanover Square. George Napoleon Epps, his half-brother, was surgeon in the same hospital and, as already mentioned, his chief work was spinal curvature, its theory and cure. William's brother Richard, (my great great grandfather) was manager of Weiss & Sons surgical instrument manufacturers at 62 The Strand and it is certainly possible that Richard's and George Epps's paths might have crossed.

John Epps was well known for his liberal views and his widow edited a collection of his diaries and notebooks, which contain two further points of connection.[190] The first relates to Italy, where it is clear that John was involved with the council of the Friends of Italy which had on its board both George Lewes and Thornton Hunt. Julia Kavanagh's letter to William's wife, of course, made reference to Roman refugees. The second relates directly to William, since he is listed in February 1836, together with Mr Ashurst, Mr Hume and Mr Hawkins, as a founder member of the Anthropological Society. This later became the Christian Phrenology Society and eventually the Anthropological Institute. This does, for me, slightly beg a question, since William had no obvious connection with anthropology except for that letter from Charles Darwin mentioned in Chapter 3. Looking further at the diary, it was a 'Mr Williams' who was listed, and in parenthesis has been added 'William Smith Williams'. Might this suggest that John Epps's widow, as editor, made the addition? It is, I acknowledge, a rather twenty-first century assumption that William may have had no involvement with anthropology, since nineteenth century thinking men and women tended not compartmentalise arts and science in the way that we do. George Lewes and George Eliot will appear in due course in William's story. Jennifer Uglow, writing about Eliot, tells how Lewes and Eliot both had a keen amateur interest in science and biology which informed their writing. [191] William certainly knew the science of lithography, so why not anthropology? Reports on scientific events appeared alongside his articles on fine arts in *The Athenaeum*. Either way, it is further evidence that William knew Epps - a name which will appear again, more than once.

November 1848 marked the start of of what would become a more regular despatch of parcels of books from Cornhill to Haworth. We don't know what was included in the November parcel but Charlotte says, 'your tastes, I thought, was recognisable in the choice of some of the volumes and a better selection it would have been difficult to make'.[192]

As we will see, the choice of books over the coming months and years was indeed interesting. I would say that at least part of William's motivation was to get this remarkable young writer to read more widely and so broaden her mind. As I have already mentioned, Margaret Smith supports this view.

Emily Brontë's health continued to deteriorate and her death on 19 December 1848 prompted from William this letter to Charlotte, which, sadly for us, appears to be the only one of his to survive:

> How to address you, my Dear Madam, on this distressing occasion I know not. To describe the astonishment and pain that the mournful intelligence has caused me, and the deep concern at the loss to her family and to the world of your

gifted sister Emily, which Mr Smith shares with me, is beyond my power. We feel for you and for your surviving - oh! what a world of sadness there is in that word! - your only sister, and for your bereaved father, and would fain shew sympathy in others ways than words, if we know how.

It was only last evening that we were talking of you, and I resolved to write, thinking fondly (what I wished) that by this time there might have been some effect produced by the medicines. How little did we imagine what was then the state of her we were anxious about! Released from pain and toil and transferred to a state of existence where her pure and exalted spirit is freed from the trammels of earth, and can look down with heavenly serenity and sympathising love, that may well pass the immeasurable distance between eternal bliss and transient sorrow, and comfort the hearts of those who mourn her departure.

To mitigate your grief for such a loss, the only way is to think of the gain to her who has been taken from you, and of the duties that now devolve upon you to support your bereaved father and comfort your sister and be comforted by her. But how superfluous it is for me to remind you of the duties that your strong sense of rectitude and energy of will prompt you to perform, and which only bodily weakness - and may God give you strength to bear this heavy affliction! - can prevent you from fulfilling. And when after the first dread shock of losing one who was your other self had passed off, and left your mind calm enough to reflect with serene sorrowful contemplation on the great and good qualities of her who is now a memory of the past and hope for the future, you cannot but find sweet consolation in recalling those noble traits of character and high intelligence for which she was distinguished: for she being dead yet liveth and speaketh. It has often occurred to me that if it were possible for us to think of our departed relatives and friends only as if they were removed to brighter world and purer sphere, and could dwell upon them our recollections of them without the disturbing medium of grief, how much more grateful and vivid and enabling would our regard and esteem for them be. But it is part of our self that is torn from us by their being snatched away, and the mortal mourns the loss of a portion of existence; while the spirit in vain strives to communicate with the departed spirit, except when directed upward. Our earthly affections, however strong and deep and pure, can only be gratified by personal intercommunion; for it is thus they are nourished; and it is for this that they are so limited, that they may refine and purify and exalt the mortal nature, and bless our daily existence with foretaste of heavenly bliss. But yet, tho' we cannot dissever our recollections of departed friends from the personal memories that recall our griefs, yet as the healing influence of time closes the wound, and deadens the pain, how sweet sad and solemn are the visions that rise to the mind when memory awakened into activity by the slightest association, peoples the world of fancy with the forms of the beloved, and the feelings of the past return with the warm glow of evening twilight before it fades into the night of oblivion.

Great griefs are life-lasting 'tis true; but their influences are as refreshing and beneficial to the soul as the night to the earth, and sleep to the body. May your night of sorrow be brief and relieved by the blessed rays of consolation that no grief is devoid of, and may the morning of peace and resignation dawn upon you both with the refreshing serenity of hopeful and affectionate feelings. You and your sister must be more and more endeared to each other now that you are left alone on earth, and having the same hopes, and sorrows, and pursuits, your sympathies will be more and more closely entwined.

God Bless and comfort you both, my dear friends, is the devout prayer of

Your sincere and attached

Wm Smith Williams[193]

The authors of the Brontë Encyclopaedia quote this only surviving letter to suggest that William had no great skill in writing and that the ambitions which frustrated him so were based more on fantasy than fact, when they say that his writing 'suggests an earlier age and does not bespeak the born writer'.[194] This letter does indeed read as somewhat laboured. It must have been a very difficult letter to write. The religious references are surely there to comfort Charlotte, rather than to reflect William's own theology. It is interesting that his writing about art is far less of a different age.

Charlotte's letter of thanks, written on Christmas Day 1848, concludes the year of the most frequent correspondence between author and reader, or, perhaps I should say, between caring friends?

8 BRONTË YEARS – CORNHILL PARCELS

William fills a gaping hole in Charlotte's life. She cannot burden her father with her worries. Her sister, Anne, is too ill either to study or read. She asks William to write to her about ordinary things. This seems to have worked, for on 1 February 1849 she is quite animated when she writes to thank him for the most recent parcel of books to arrive. However, it seems that I might not have been entirely correct in my assessment of William's motivation in sending the book boxes, for Charlotte reports that 'Papa is at the moment reading Macaulay's *History* and Anne is engaged with one of Fredrika Bremer's *Tales*'.[195]

The books, it seems, fulfilled many functions. Margaret Smith suggests that, through the medium of the book boxes that William sent to Haworth, he was in effect offering Charlotte a window on the world - a course in liberal arts.[196] Smith goes on to explain the modules on offer. History and Sociology came through Macaulay's *History of England*, Charles Kingsley's *Alton Locke* and Leigh Hunt's *The Town*; International Society and Culture through Julia Kavanagh's *Madeleine* and *Women in France* and Thackeray's *Paris Sketch Book,* and George Borrow's *The Bible in Spain*; Women's Studies came through the writings of Mrs Ellis but more so through *Thoughts on Self-Culture Addressed to Women* by Maria Grey and Emily Shirreff. We have already seen that William himself far more than ably tackled the Art module. I would add that Politics was also not losing out, being covered by Thomas Carlyle's writings.

In her letter, Charlotte goes on to say that she is enclosing the first volume of her next work, *Shirley*, and to seek his opinion. In barely a week, William responds with the frank comments that she had requested, but goes on to reject. On 4 February, she writes again to say that the parcel containing *Shirley* has been sent, but that 'the manuscript has all its errors upon it not having been read through since copying'. She goes on to talk about the content of the parcel that William had sent. She writes of Julia Kavanagh with both respect and affection. She had read Emerson's *Essays* with 'much interest and often admiration, but they are of mined gold and clay – deep and invigorating truth – dreary and depressing fallacy seem to me combined therein.' She loved George Borrow and wrote 'after reading *The Bible in Spain* I felt as if I have travelled at his side'.[197]

The letters from Charlotte that follow are inevitably overshadowed by, now, Anne's illness, which grows steadily worse; and, once again, William commends homoeopathy and, once again, it is rejected. Charlotte though is pressing on with her second book, as emerges from her letter of 2 April.

> My critics truly deserve and have my genuine thanks for the friendly candour with which they have declared their opinions on my book. Both Mr. Williams and Mr. Taylor express and support their opinions in a manner calculated to command careful consideration. In my turn I have a word to say. You both of you dwell too

much on what you regard as the artistic treatment of a subject. Say what you will, gentlemen — say it as ably as you will — truth is better than art. Burns' Songs are better than Bulwer's Epics. Thackeray's rude, careless sketches are preferable to thousands of carefully finished paintings. Ignorant as I am, I dare to hold and maintain that doctrine. [198]

I hope a further authorial interjection might be permitted here, for in the Smith, Elder & Co. archive in the National Library of Scotland are some of Thackeray's rough sketches and they are, indeed, a total delight.

Charlotte's letter continues with comment on the characters in *Shirley*, a first draft of which she had sent with her letter of 1 February. She asks for the manuscript to be returned, we assume, for amendment.

Her letter of 16 April comes to life as Charlotte tells of the books that she has been reading from the Cornhill boxes. They are all from Smith, Elder & Co.'s list. The first was by Alexander Harris, *The Emigrant Family*, about the experience of emigrating to Australia - a subject that would later resonate personally with William. Charlotte enjoyed it, but not as much as his first book, *Testimony to the Truth*, which had contained religious views that had resonated strongly. Leigh Hunt's *The Town* had delighted her with its anecdotes of London. Carlyle she likes more and more, but, again, not his writing style.

30 May brought the news that William was dreading: Anne had died whilst she and Charlotte were away at Scarborough. Charlotte writes, 'I let Anne go to God and felt He had a right to her'. Nearly a fortnight later she continues, 'You have been kind enough to take a certain interest in my afflictions, and I feel a sort of duty to tell you how I am enabled to sustain them'. She had lost her three siblings in the course of a year and she concludes that 'there must be Heaven or we must despair – for life seems bitter, brief, blank'. She continues, 'To me these two

have left in their memories a noble legacy [....] there is something in the past I can love intensely and honour deeply [...] They have died comparatively young – but their sort lives were spotless – their brief career was honourable – their untimely death befell amidst all association that can hallow, and not one that can desecrate.[199]

This striking phrase was picked up in a piece by Mabel Edgerley from *The Brontës Then and Now* in which she says, 'surely this one of the most beautiful letters ever written by Charlotte. It was sent to Mr Williams shortly after Anne's death.'

Charlotte returned home, to a Haworth sadly changed:

W.S. Williams,

June 25th, 1849

My dear Sir,

I am now again at home where I returned last Thursday. I call it home still – much as London would be called London if an earthquake should shake its streets to ruins. But let me not be ungrateful: Haworth parsonage is still a home for me, and not quite a ruined or desolate home either. Papa is there – and two more affectionate and faithful servants - and two old dogs, in their way as faithful and affectionate – Emily's large house dog which lay at the side of her dying-bed and followed her funeral to the vault, lying in the pew couched at our feet while the burial service was being read – and Anne's little spaniel. The ecstasy of these poor animals when I came in was something singular –a farmer returns from brief absence – They always welcomed me warmly – but not in that strange, heart-touching way.[200]

Her letter continues with a lament at loneliness. There is a post-script to thank William for the most recent book parcel, albeit coloured with sadness at her memory of

Emily's enjoyment of them. I read this letter in Charlotte's handwriting in the library at Haworth. I could almost sense the presence of the dogs and the dreadful sadness.

She next writes having been cheered by further parcels of books, and convinced that 'labour is the only cure for rooted sorrow'. Concerned about William, she finishes, 'Mrs Williams should spare herself for her husband's and children's sake – her life and health are too valuable to those round her to be lavished – she should be careful of them'.[201] It was the following year that Julia Kavanagh wrote to Margaret Williams about the plight of Roman refugees, I wonder whether Margaret, in the middle of 1849, was taking up worthy causes at a cost to her health. William, once again, writes of his daughters. His letter seems to have been well judged for Charlotte replies on 3 July, 1849

> You do right to address me on subjects which compel me, in order to give a coherent answer, to quit for a moment my habitual train of thought. The mention of your healthy living daughters reminds me of the world where other people live – where I lived once. Theirs are cheerful images – as you present them: I have no wish to shut them out.[202]

Of Ellen she says, 'I esteem a dutiful daughter who makes her parents happy'. Of Fanny, she reserves judgement and certainly is disinclined to take William's word. Louisa has a chance of a place at Queen's College and Charlotte is full of encouragement, adding, 'Whenever I have seen families of daughters sitting waiting to be married, I have pitied them from my heart.' William has mentioned, again, the family home at Broxbourne and Charlotte recalls how he had done so a year before and how then she would talk about his letters. 'Now I read them – return them to their covers and put them away'. She concludes with words of solace:

> Lonely as I am – how should I be if Providence had never given me courage to adopt a career – perseverance to plead through two long, weary years with publishers till they admitted me? How should I be with youth past – sisters lost – a resident in a moorland parish where there is not a single educated family? In that case I should have no world at all. [203]

In relation to Louisa, Margaret Smith tells that she obtained from the college copies of her first class certificates in French and Mathematics signed in 1853.[204] In 1849 Louisa was only embarking on her studies there, and, in July 1849, far from certain of obtaining a place as Charlotte tells her friend Ellen Nussey in her letter of 4 July. George Smith was 'kindly using his influence to obtain votes'. Charlotte's reply to William also allows us to infer that his wife's health problems might have been resolved.

> Truly glad was I to hear of your daughter's success. I trust its results may conduce to the permanent advantage both of herself and her parents.
>
> Of still more importance than your children's education is your wife's health and therefore it is still more gratifying to learn that your anxiety on that account is likely to be alleviated.
>
> For her own sake - no less than for that of others - it is to be hoped that she is now secured from a recurrence of her painful and dangerous attacks. It was pleasing too, to hear of good qualities being developed in the daughters by the mother's danger. May your girls always so act as to justify their father's kind estimate of their characters; may they never do what might disappoint or grieve him.

Charlotte continues, responding to what was surely a kindly thought from William, but which sheds light on her daily life:

> Your suggestion relative to myself is a good one in some respects, but there are two persons whom it would not suit; and not the least incommoded of these would be the young person whom I might request to come and bury herself in the hills of Haworth, to take a church and stony churchyard for her prospect, the dead silence of a village parsonage — in which the tick of the clock is heard all day long — for her atmosphere, and a grave, silent spinster for her companion. I should not like to see youth thus immured. The hush and gloom of our house would be more oppressive to a buoyant than to a subdued spirit. The fact is, my work is my best companion; hereafter I look for no great earthly comfort except what congenial occupation can give. For society, long seclusion has in a great measure un-fitted me, I doubt whether I should enjoy it if I might have it. Sometimes I think I should, and I thirst for it; but at other times I doubt my capability of pleasing or deriving pleasure. The prisoner in solitary confinement, the toad in the block of marble, all in time shape themselves to their lot. —
>
> Yours sincerely, C. Brontë.[205]

The mention of Queen's College brings a further name into William's story, that of F.D. Maurice. He was a well known Christian socialist, much admired by Charlotte Brontë as indicated in her letter to James Taylor of 15 November 1851; she had heard him preach on her trip to London that summer. Queen's College in London's Harley Street was founded in 1848 by F.D. Maurice with 'active help from his colleagues at King's College London and of his Cambridge friends, and with direct encouragement of Queen Victoria'. Words, written by Maurice's son in the foreword to a short history of the college, highlight its status. Notwithstanding this, it was met with a wall of prejudice and ridicule - for example in Gilbert and Sullivan's *Princess Ida*. The history goes on to explain that Maurice's initiative had stemmed from concern at the then low educational standards of governesses - a subject that resonates strongly in Charlotte's correspondence with William.[206] It was very much part of the origin of the movements that would eventually demand votes and equality for women. The history was written very much with the view that women had their place.

FD Maurice founded not only Queen's College, but also the Working Men's College, together with John Ruskin and Lowes Dickinson. These foundations were massively more than the name F.D. Maurice; they represented a revolution in many ways as big as any of those others which William had encountered in his life. Education (what we would term tertiary education) was being made available to working men and to women. That the latter should find a place in a chapter on Charlotte Brontë makes every possible sense. A good deal of the correspondence between Charlotte and William concerned the lot of women - young women in particular who, in the opinions of both of them, should be able to make their own way in the world without being dependent upon a husband. The availability of education at the right level and of the right quality was fundamental to this. In her paper, 'Female Education as a Theme in the Novels of Charlotte Brontë', Margaret Mills supports this by arguing that:

> In her novels, Charlotte Brontë challenges the experiences of women in education, class, marriage and employment. It is not surprising that female education had a prominent part to play in her novels: two of them have their main setting within a school, and the protagonist is

employed as teacher, governess or tutor. Although Charlotte's preoccupation with teaching as a career and with the means by which a woman could achieve that role reflects her own life experience, it is incorrect to assume that she wrote about these matters simply because this was familiar territory for her. Education, and particularly the education of women, was an issue of growing importance in the eighteenth and nineteenth centuries.[207]

For a justification of the mention of the Working Men's College, we need look no further than Charlotte's book, *Shirley*, on which she was working that summer. Also, as Juliet Barker points out, Charlotte would have seen the hard lot of working men in her own village of Haworth.[208] The string upon which the story of *Shirley* hangs is the revolution taking place in industry, where machinery is massively increasing the productivity of men and also removing low-skilled jobs and replacing them with those demanding of higher skills. The workers in *Shirley* didn't see it that way; they believed that machines were robbing them of their jobs.

The Mechanics Institutes and equivalent bodies around the country had, for twenty years or so, been giving working men the opportunity to learn the skills that they would need in the new industrial world. The Working Men's College was different. It didn't lecture; it taught. Maurice believed that if 'knowledge and culture, science and literature are any good, that good apart from any trace of utility'.[209] The Working Men's College, first at Red Lion Square and then in Great Ormond Street, became another nexus for William's artist friends. In 1854 F.D. Maurice, who was then the Chaplain of Lincoln's Inn and Dean of King's College, conceived the idea of a college, largely through the means of evening classes, which would bring education within the reach of working men. The booklet produced on the foundation of the college notes that the

Reform Act of 1832 had done nothing for working men and it was only the subsequent reform in 1867 that broadened the suffrage to include householders who rented rather than owned their property.[210] There had been a great deal of agitation for a clear voice for the working man. Those offering education at the college included John Ruskin but also Ford Madox Brown, Edward Burn Jones, Dante Gabriel Rossetti and Lowes Dickinson, who, the booklet states, taught there for some sixteen years. One of Dickinson's many portraits was of Maurice. Of Ruskin's involvement, the author of the booklet writes, 'It helped the enterprise as a whole by letting the world know that one of the greatest Englishmen of the time was in active sympathy with it'. It is clear that Ruskin was thoroughly active in the project. He taught sketching and mentored a number of his students, one of whom (George Allen) would, much later, become his publisher. A further name that appears in the Working Men's College is that of Charles Kingsley, then a clergyman, he who would go on to write *Alton Locke* and also *The Water Babies* with all its Darwinian imagery.

William would have to wait for the end of the summer of 1849 for Charlotte to complete the manuscript of *Shirley*. When writing this paragraph, I had in front of me Charlotte's letter to William of 24 August 1849 and I was in the Brontë Parsonage where she wrote it. She begins, 'I think the best title for the book would be "Shirley" without any explanation as addition – the simpler and briefer, the better.'[211] In the remainder of the letter she suggests that Mr Taylor comes to Haworth to collect the Manuscript. This is followed by a long excuse why she has not invited William to Haworth and why she suggests Mt Taylor only visits for a day. It revolves round Papa whose custom is to be solitary. Writing in the parsonage, I had a strong sense of father and daughter and their solitary life.

In her letter to William of 29 August she reports that manuscript is ready for James Taylor to collect adding that she is unable to tell whether it is better or worse than *Jane Eyre*. A sticking point proved to be the preface which William urged Charlotte to change. Her refusal eventually meant that *Shirley* was published without preface but also, perhaps, that her letters to William began to cool. James Taylor was undertaking the editing of the book, but it was to William that Charlotte wrote with her refusal to make changes.

William persisted with his efforts to get her to change the preface, but eventually in her letter of 17 September, it is clear that he has given her the approbation she seeks:

> An author who has shown his book to none, held no consultation about plan, subject, characters or incidents, asked and had no opinion from one living being, but fabricated it darkly in the silent workshop of his own brain – such an author awaits with a singular feeling the report of the first impression produced by his creation in a quarter where he places confidence, and truly glad when that report proves favourable.[212]

Shirley was published by Smith, Elder & Co. and Charlotte's letter of 5 November thanks William for forwarding reviews. He obviously advised her to 'preserve her equanimity'. That from *The Examiner* she liked. 'I am willing to be judged by the Examiner – I like the Examiner. Fonblanque has power, he has discernment – I bend to his censorship, I am grateful for his praise; his blame deserves consideration; when he approves, I permit myself a moderate promotion of pride'.[213]

In *The Athenaeum* the annotation isn't entirely clear, but it could well have been Dilke himself who wrote a long and detailed review. He begins by praising the author for their hard work in portraying a world closer to reality than *Jane Eyre*. But this is as far as his praise goes. It is clear that he can't quite understand why *Jane Eyre* had been so well received; it was not, in his view, anything to do with the art of the writer, who he is convinced is a woman. He concludes by saying, 'We do not think that *Shirley* is an advance on *Jane Eyre*: - and, without prophesying its ultimate destiny, we imagine that it is a book which women will admire as very passionate and which men may regard as somewhat prosy'.[214]

Shirley perhaps didn't gain the public acclaim that met *Jane Eyre*, but it does explore issues that were at the forefront of people's minds and draws on Charlotte's own experience of working with clergy, working as a governess and moving in the company of people from many parts of Yorkshire society. It does, I think, also draw on the Cornhill books. It is set at the time of the Napoleonic Wars and it is surely possible to detect Carlyle's writing on the French Revolution. The political detail of the impact of Napoleon on Britain forms a key driver of the plot, with the often-repeated reference to the Orders in Council, which decimated the textile trade and caused so much suffering to the characters. There is lively debate about the tensions of industrialisation, and possibly most there is a deep exploration of the role of women. It is a moot point whether this latter debate was informed by the Cornhill books or came directly from Charlotte's own experience.

A further name in William's story is found in Charlotte's letter to him of 17 November. He had sent to her a letter from Elizabeth Gaskell. Charlotte was aware, when she submitted *Shirley* to her publishers, that the anonymously written *Mary Barton* was about very much the same subject area. The identity of its author soon became clear and was of course Mrs Gaskell. With this letter as its starting point, a friendship would grow between the two women which would, tragically, reach fruition with Elizabeth writing Charlotte's biography following her untimely death.

It is clear from a number of letters that Charlotte had made a visit to London. On 5 December she writes to Ellen Nussey from Paddington of the kindness shown by her hostess, Mrs Smith, of her liking for George Smith and of her doubts about James Taylor who, she says, 'rules the firm...and keeps 40 young men under strict control.' She adds that, 'Mr Williams too is really most gentlemanly and well-informed – his weak points certainly he has – but these are not seen in society'.[215] On the same day she writes a letter to her father about meeting Thackeray, in which she also tells of a visit to the National Gallery and a 'beautiful' exhibition of Mr Turner's paintings. In a letter to Margaret Wooler on 14 February 1850, Jian Choe writes that, Charlotte recalls: 'Nothing charmed me more during my stay in Town than the pictures I saw — one or two private collections of Turner's best water-colour drawings were indeed a treat: his later oil-paintings are strange things — things that baffle description'.

Choe continues, 'Charlotte Brontë's puzzled reaction here revealed was typical of public opinion on Turner's later so-called 'eccentric' pictures. The radically new style of art that he evolved towards the end of his life was, being far ahead of his time, unintelligible to his contemporaries'.[216] William certainly admired Turner's early work; there is no evidence one way or another on his views on the 'eccentric' pictures. Having said that, William's writing on colour and light in his *John Bull* article might suggest a sympathy with late Turner.

Four days later, Charlotte writes, again, in anticipation of meeting Miss Martineau, another celebrated writer on social issues, who had responded warmly to *Jane Eyre*. She also reports that Mr Williams had taken her round the new Houses of Parliament at a time when the young Pugin was supervising the wood carving.[217]

Probably the high point of Charlotte's London visit was a dinner. This was hosted by George Smith and his guests included the critics of *The Times*, *The Athenaeum*, *The Examiner*, *The Spectator* and *The Atlas* with probably both Thackeray and William: 'Men more dreaded in the world of letters than you can conceive,' she writes to Laetitia

Wheelwright. 'I did not know how much their presence and conversation had excited me until they were gone, and then the reaction commenced. When I retired for the night I wished to sleep – the effort to do so was in vain – I could not close my eyes'.[218]

A journey back to Haworth and a few days to reflect put her in the mood, once again, to write to William, first addressing his request for her further opinion on his daughters. Slightly in parenthesis, I wonder whether this request has an echo from *Shirley*, where the narrator offers almost uncomfortably frank comment on the Yorke family, and the children in particular. Charlotte is at pains to stress that, on the evidence of one evening, only an impression could be given. 'They impressed me then as pleasing in manners and appearance: Ellen's is a character to which I could soon attach myself and Fanny and Louisa have each their separate advantages. I can however read more in a face like Mrs Williams' than in the smooth young features of her daughters – Time, Trial and Exertion write a distinct hand more legible than smile and dimple'.[219] Charlotte goes on to offer comments on the thoughts of Fanny becoming a professional singer. She cautions, 'there should be no urging, no goading'. Her final comments are reserved for the critics whom she met. She rather liked Chorley of *The Athenaeum*. When I was leafing through the annotated copies, it was Chorley's name that kept appearing.

William has expressed wonder at the 'infrequency of sincere attachments among women' and has asked Charlotte if she should write to Mrs Williams. Charlotte's first letter of 1850 addresses this wonder and ends with the counter-suggestion that Mrs Williams should write to her first:

> You allude to the subject of female friendships and express wonder at the infrequency of sincere attachments amongst women. As to married women, I can well understand that they should

be absorbed in their husbands and children – but single women often like each other much and desire great solace from their mutual regard. Friendship however is a plant which cannot be forced – true friendship is no gourd springing up in the night and withering in a day.[220]

The letter focusses on Charlotte's friendship with Ellen, and she explains that she would have replied before had she not been spending all day talking to Ellen, whose 'society makes [her] indolent and negligent'.

As to William's wonder, the Williams house was small and household large, and he was surely much engaged elsewhere. I question whether he would know of any female friendships which his wife enjoyed. As to the letter writing or, more accurately non-letter writing between Charlotte and Margaret, is William missing what to me seems obvious? Surely these are two women who are suspicious of each other.

Just one week later, Charlotte is back to reviews and is clearly stung by what G.H. Lewes had to say about *Shirley* in the Edinburgh Review. 'I am not angry with Mr Lewes – but I wish in future he would leave me alone'. She, though, does not leave him alone and writes to Lewes on 19 January asking to be judged as an author not as a woman. William is, of course, caught in the middle, having been the route by which Lewes could give such a positive review of *Jane Eyre* two years earlier. Her next letter is not until 22 February and in it she asks to be sent two more novels of Jane Austen, having thus far only read *Pride and Prejudice*.

The letter of 16 March opens a little window on the Williams family. Margaret's father has died and, not unnaturally, Margaret is mourning. It is Richard, then aged eleven, who seems to be suffering the most from the loss of his grandfather, Francis Hill, headmaster of Broxbourne School. It doesn't seem that William makes any reference to the early loss of his own parents. Many years later an article was written setting out memories of the school in Broxbourne and of its headmaster which might indicate that there was one Francis at school and quite a different one at home with his grandchildren:

> School being duly entered the day scholars took the south, the boarders the north side. Work was commenced under the genial eye of old Francis Hill, the dominie and church clerk, but much cannot be said for the work done, though the boys got on fairly well, and discipline was maintained by free use of the cane and the well-known and much dreaded strap and buckle, and other effective punishments long since abolished (wisely or not we will not say). On Wednesdays and Fridays in Lent and other feasts of the church, the dominie would be seen making his toilet at the back of the desk, his presence being required at the church to read the responses. During his absence the old adage fully applied "While the cat is away the mice will play". His return was the signal for renewed industry and energy, or the appearance of it.[221]

The memory was from 1838 and Francis's daughter is shown as assisting him.

On the same day, 16 March, Charlotte writes to Thornton Hunt declining his invitation to become a contributor to the magazine he was launching with G.H. Lewes entitled *The Leader,* to which Harriet Martineau and other free thinkers had agreed to contribute. There is nothing to say that Charlotte knew of the rather unconventional way that Lewes and Hunt chose to live. Just one month after Charlotte's letter was written, Lewes's wife gave birth to Edmund whose father was Thornton Hunt. Eighteen months later, on 21 October 1851 their second child Rose was born. Lewes registered both children as his own in order to protect them.[222] Bryan

Courthorpe Leigh Hunt was born to Agnes on 6 January 1852, Ethel Isabella Lewes on 9 October 1853 and Beatrice Mary Leigh Hunt on 16 November 1853. A final child, Mildred Jane Lewes, was born to Thornton and Agnes on 21 May 1857.[223] George Lewes, Agnes and Thornton Hunt believed in open marriage. George also found his way to live out his beliefs. On 6 October 1851, in Jeffs Bookshop in the Burlington Arcade, he met Mary Ann Evans who was working as a largely unpaid assistant editor at *The Westminster Review*. Lewes had recently published a very popular *Biographical History of Philosophy* and was becoming increasingly well know in literary circles.[224] George and Mary Ann, otherwise known as George Eliot, soon began living together as man and wife, and they would do so until 1878 when Lewes died. There is no record of what William or his wife thought about all this. William, certainly, continued his friendship with both Lewes and Hunt, and indeed with George Eliot as I explore in Chapter 10.

Book parcels return to the heart of correspondence, with William providing Charlotte with nourishing fare including Southey's *Life*, *Women in France* by Julia Kavanagh (covering many of the most prominent contemporary French women), Hazlitt's *Essays*, Emerson's *Representative Men* (covering Plato, Montaigne, Shakespeare, Napoleon and Goethe) and Scott's *Suggestions on Female Education*. The latter she particularly liked. Charlotte makes no comment about Southey, but she would surely remember his father's cruel rejection in 1837 when she sent to the then Poet Laureate some of her poems. Rebecca Fraser records Southey as having written:

> You evidently possess, and in no inconsiderable degree, that Wordsworth calls "the faculty of verse" [....] Literature cannot be the business of a woman's life, and it ought not to be [...] the daydreams in which you habitually indulge are likely to induce a distempered state of mind'.[225]

Margaret Smith includes, in her edition of Charlotte's letters, a list of the books that Smith Elder & Co. has sent to Haworth. A number of these have been referred to elsewhere in Charlotte's letters. Of the remainder, I noticed the *Letters* of Charles Lamb, which have their echo back with Taylor & Hessey.

Another book in the list was described as 'Self-Culture', and it has already been mentioned. Margaret Smith suggests that this quite probably was *Thoughts on Self-Culture, addressed to Women* by Maria Grey and her sister Emily Shirreff, both of whom championed women's education. Grey founded a college for female teachers and wrote on women's suffrage. Shirreff supported the founding of Girton College. Books continue as the subject of her letter of 12 April and Charlotte offers views on Jane Austen:

> I have likewise read one of Miss Austen's works — Emma — read it with interest and with just the degree of admiration which Miss Austen herself would have thought sensible and suitable. Anything like warmth or enthusiasm — anything energetic, poignant, heart-felt is utterly out of place in commending these works: all such demonstration the authoress would have met with a well-bred sneer, would have calmly scorned as outré and extravagant. She does her business of delineating the surface of the lives of genteel English people curiously well. There is a Chinese fidelity, a miniature delicacy in the painting. She ruffles her reader by nothing vehement, disturbs him by nothing profound. The passions are perfectly unknown to her; she rejects even a speaking acquaintance with that stormy sisterhood. Even to the feelings she vouchsafes no more than an occasional graceful but distant recognition — too frequent converse with them would ruffle the smooth elegance of her progress.

Her business is not half so much with the human heart as with the human eyes, mouth, hands, and feet. What sees keenly, speaks aptly, moves flexibly, it suits her to study; but what throbs fast and full, though hidden, what the blood rushes through, what is the unseen seat of life and the sentient target of death — this Miss Austen ignores. She no more, with her mind's eye, beholds the heart of her race than each man, with bodily vision, sees the heart in his heaving breast. Jane Austen was a complete and most sensible lady, but a very incomplete and rather insensible (not senseless) woman. If this is heresy, I cannot help it. If I said it to some people (Lewes for instance) they would directly accuse me of advocating exaggerated heroics, but I am not afraid of your falling into any such vulgar error. — Believe me, yours sincerely, C. Brontë.[226]

William may have smiled at her closing comment, 'Jane Austen was a complete and most sensible lady. But a very incomplete and rather insensible woman'.[227]

William has, it seems, expressed a longing 'for liberty and leisure', and Charlotte offers sympathy in her letter of 22 May. William had a traditional job and a traditional family but he had, among his friends, some very untraditional people doing quite untraditional things. We might today call it a mid-life crisis. There was perhaps another reason for William's disquiet.

William Rossetti recalled that an article William had written for *The Spectator* had so offended that the aggrieved person, a watercolour artist, threatened to sue. I have read the art criticism in *The Spectator* for that summer and much is robust. However, I couldn't tell which was written by William and which was the offending piece. In his reminiscences, Rossetti is equally unable to recall the detail, save that William was looking for someone to take his place. Rossetti tells how, in the October of that year,

William was at the house of Lowes Dickinson and the two were discussing the matter. Madox Brown, who was also present, came up with the suggestion of William Rossetti. Rossetti subsequently visited William at his 'very small house', with his 'very large family'. William he found, 'well turned of forty years, a pleasant spoken man, with an open countenance and fine crop of hair.' Rossetti then met with Rintoul and began his career as a writer 'otherwise than gratis'.[228]

In the art world of 1850, this was but a small storm in a tea cup. In contrast, *The Spectator's* review of the Royal Academy Exhibition in the edition of 4 May 1850 contained a few sentences on two artists whose impact on nineteenth century British painting would be massive.

> In this room the two most singular pictures are, a design of the young Jesus, by Millais, and "A Converted British Family Sheltering a Christian Missionary from the persecution of the Druids", by WH Hunt – leading types of the Pre-Raphaelite school: both are full of ability, especially that by Millais, both monstrously perverse, Millais still being the greater culprit. If one can penetrate through the nonsense of the manner to which is really in the artist, he may be conjectured to possess more power than any man in the place: but a painter who can spontaneously go back, not to the perfect schools, but through and beyond them to the days of puerile crudity, seems likely to be conscious of some fatal constitutional disease in his genius or he would hardly, in malice prepense, make deliberate choice of impotency.

A review such as this must have reverberated around the circle of those supporting the Brotherhood including William, whose family relationship with the Pre-Raphaelites was really quite strong. Angela Thirlwell's's book *William and Lucy, The Other Rossettis,* about William and Lucy, who was Madox Brown's daughter, refers to Lowes Dickinson giving them a wedding present. It also mentions a party thrown by Dr John Epps and tells how William Rossetti danced with Nellie Epps; she later married Edmund Gosse and was the sister of Emily Epps our William's daughter-in-law. Later correspondence between Robert Hill and his sister suggests that the Rossettis were known to the wider Hill family.[229]

Painting, again, figured when Charlotte visited London at the beginning of June. Writing to Ellen Nussey on 3 June 1850, she reports that she too had seen the Royal Academy Exhibition, but passes no comment. The same report in her letter to her father of the following day adds how much she admired Landseer's Duke of Wellington on the field of Waterloo. Perhaps her admiration for the Iron Duke began to hold sway over any sympathy with the more revolutionary thinking espoused by William?

9 BRONTË YEARS – A COOLING

On 12 June 1850 Charlotte writes to Ellen Nussey to report on meetings with Thackeray, Lewes and Julia Kavanagh. She then says this:

> I have seen considerably more of the Williams family but would rather communicate my impressions in conversation than by writing - Mr Williams, his three daughters and his son where here at a ball Mrs Smith gave last Friday - the ease and grace, the natural gentility of the manners of all five were remarkable - their dress - their appearance were decoration to the rooms - as Mrs Smith afterwards remarked - I called on their house yesterday and I can hardly tell why I came away much pained - others do not see – or at least do not mention - what I seem to see in that family - whether I am partly mistaken I do not know. Mrs Williams had been here too - her conversation is most fluent and intelligent - her manners perfectly good - of her character - in a moral point of view I can have no doubts - and yet I confess there is something about all

excepting the father himself and the eldest daughter from which I feel inclined to shrink.[230]

This brought to my mind Margaret Williams's comment as recalled by Anna after a visit by the Brontë sisters; there was surely a degree of suspicion between the two ladies. I do wonder, though, whether this marked the point when Charlotte began to step back a little from her friendship with William. Charlotte's next letter to him of 20 July has no hint of any reservation in her feelings; they were to be kept strictly between Charlotte and her friend.

William might have detected a hint of cooling in Charlotte's letter of 27 August. Again, I am quoting from the original. William has asked once again for her advice about his daughter who, it seems, is considering taking a position as a governess to a family in Italy. Charlotte says:

> So much of the matter depends on the character of her who is principally concerned that, I think, herself alone and those to whom she is intimately known can judge the eligibility or ineligibility of the plan. To all English girls a residence as governess in a foreign family and land must be a trial: to the firm-principled, healthy and self-reliant it may be a trial terminating in gain; to the more pliable, delicate and dependent all might prove [unrepaired] suffering. [231]

The letter continues with a report of Charlotte's visit to the Lakes and Sir J.K. Shuttleworth with a lament that she couldn't enjoy any solitude. There is then reference to a visit to Mrs Gaskell and a rather frank comment about William's friend George Lewes:

> I had some days' enjoyment of her society: I like her much: her manner is kind, cordial and unassuming, and her conversation peculiarly interesting. She told me sundry things regarding

Mr Lewes which prove that he has by no means a proper regard for the strict truth, nor indeed much scruple at throwing out of inventions. He is a very vexatious and rather naughty little man.

On 5 September, Charlotte writes this time warming to William's suggestion of a new edition of *Wuthering Heights* and *Agnes Grey* with a preface from herself. The next couple of letters wrestle with Newby's copyright. The draft preface arrives with William on 20 September and a week later some more material, resulting in a draft of the new edition: *Wuthering Heights & Agnes Grey by E&A Bell With a Notice of the Authors by Currer Bell and a Selection of their Literary Remains.*

It seems that, again, there is a disagreement over the wording of the preface. A resolution is found and, in her letter of 16 October, Charlotte courteously accepts William's suggestion.

The breadth of genre and subject covered by the books that William is sending up to Haworth grows with each parcel. In her letter of 25 October 1850, Charlotte writes of Jeffrey's *Essays*, Dr Arnold's *Life*, Charles Kingsley's *Alton Locke,* Macaulay's *Essays*, Sidney Smith's *Lectures on Moral Philosophy*, Knox and Pilgrim's work on race, Leigh Hunt's autobiography and Hazlitt's *Essays*. William is also moving further afield than Smith Elder & Co.'s own publications. Macaulay was the very much establishment historian and Charles Kingsley, the Christian socialist, was a man whose views concurred with much of what Carlyle was also writing.

The religious theme continues into Charlotte's letter of 9 November when the feared resurgence of Roman Catholicism through the Anglo-Catholics had been in the press. Charlotte's interest in and concern about Julia Kavanagh resurfaces. She also writes with great enthusiasm about R.H. Horne's *Death of Marlowe*.

Charlotte writes to William on New Year's Day 1851 to thank him for further parcels of books, with the words 'you are all very – very good'. In the same letter, she touches on two relationships which are becoming more and more important. She asks William to send a copy of *Wuthering Heights* to Mrs Gaskell. She then writes warmly of her meeting with Harriet Martineau. Back in 1849, Charlotte had asked William to send to Martineau a copy of *Shirley*. Margaret Smith suggests that Harriet Martineau made her name through her 'well-informed *Illustrations of Political Economy*'. She goes on to say that Martineay differed in many ways from Charlotte, but, in the end, they shared the same message: 'When will it be understood by all that it rests with all to bring about a time when opposition of interests shall cease? When will masters and men work cheerfully together for the common good, respect instead of proscribing each other?'[232]

William, I would expect, had much sympathy with these views, although I can find no direct contact between him and Martineau. Nevertheless, there is, in the Smith Elder & Co. archive, an undated letter from Martineau to George Smith talking about *Villette* and Thackeray's *Henry Esmond*. Harriet Martineau was one of 1,521 signatories in the 1866 petition to Parliament for the extension of the suffrage to women.[233]

William continues in his care for Charlotte, making no attempt to pressurise her into writing a third novel. He had also written to her father to similar effect. William was, as ever, keenly aware of her fragile state. After this, there are no further letter to William until 21 July 1851.

In her letter to George Smith of 19 April 1851, Charlotte writes, 'Please tell Mr Williams that I dare on no account come to London till he is friends with me, which I am sure he cannot be, as I have never heard from him for nearly three months.' Margaret Smith explains the gap in correspondence by noting that Thackeray had given the firm 'dreadful trouble' with his lack of punctuality over his next book.[234] When William eventually wrote, he said that 'if Smith had not helped him out with his "vigour energy and method", he must have sunk under the day & night labour of the last few weeks'.[235] The first of Thackeray's novels to be published by Smith, Elder & Co. had been *The Kickleburys on the Rhine*, a Christmas book for 1850, and which had proved a success.[236] Thackeray would go on to have a significant involvement with the firm. William's time may also have been taken up by Volume 1 of John Ruskin's *Stones of Venice* which appeared in 1851, accompanied by *Examples of the Architecture of Venice*.

Charlotte mentions in a letter to George Smith of 12 May, that she is looking forward to seeing Mr Williams. I can't help sensing from these rather oscillating emotions that there is very clearly still a friendship between William and Charlotte, with the ups and downs that friendships so often have. In that same letter of 12 May, Charlotte strongly condemns Mr Thackeray for his negative comments about Ruskin. A positive review of *The Stones of Venice* appeared in *The Examiner* of 12 April. We can, perhaps, imagine many conversations taking place on this subject, where Ruskin is questioning accepted wisdom. Meanwhile, there was another subject generating even more controversy.

A Great Exhibition at the Crystal Palace, celebrating industrial advances, had been promoted from July 1849 by Prince Albert and Sir Henry Cole - the same man who had encouraged William in his paper on lithography. It was the cause of many and long arguments. Some people, such as Ruskin, had serious reservations about the benefits of industry. Others were writing about its very clear disadvantages, in terms of urban poverty. All strands of industry, from both Great Britain and elsewhere, were to exhibit their wares. In the early part of 1851, Richard Williams, William's brother, was acting as secretary to the group of surgical instrument makers preparing their displays for the Great Exhibition. He was running the office of Weiss & Son at 62 The Strand. For the exhibition, Weiss had produced a most marvellous instrument comprising 1851 knives.

With kind permission of John Weiss & Sons

This was clearly a bit of showing off. Yet, behind the scenes, advances were being made in surgery, through the work of Joseph Lister and others, and the makers of instruments took up the challenge to keep pace.

Charlotte Brontë's relationship with the Exhibition was, perhaps, characteristic. On 17 April 1851, she wrote to George Smith's mother to say, 'I was nursing a comfortable and complacent conviction that I had quite made up my mind not to go to London this year: the Great Exhibition was nothing – only a series of bazaars under a magnified hothouse'.[237] She did, however, go, as she wrote to her father on 31 May 1851 'Yesterday we went to the Crystal Palace – the exterior has a strange and elegant but somewhat unsubstantial effect – The interior is like a mighty Vanity Fair - the brightest colours blaze on all sides – and ware of all kinds – from diamonds to spinning jennies and Printing Presses are there to be seen – It was very fine – gorgeous – animated – bewildering'.[238]

CHARLOTTE BRONTË'S DEVOTEE

The Great Exhibition drew both great praise and harsh criticism. A wonderful series of lithographs were produced by Lowes Dickinson's firm and they are available for us to see on the British Library website.[239]

William's relationship with this major national event is not documented. His nephew Alfred Hamlyn Williams was, by then, twenty years old and, in the course of his career, would register a number of patents for inventions that he had made. Surely, he would have visited, not least given his father's participation. The involvement of Lowes Dickinson might suggest a visit by William's daughter, Ellen, even though they wouldn't marry for a further six years. This involvement and William's earlier connection with Henry Cole (through his paper *On Lithography*) would certainly suggest to me that William himself would have visited.

We now know that throughout her visits, *Villette* was very much taking shape in Charlotte's mind, and possibly, too, on paper. In her letter to William of 21 July, which follows her visits, she first explains that she had delayed replying to his long and interesting letter until the box (the Cornhill parcel of books) reached her. She tells him that 'these Cornhill-parcels have something of the magic charm of a fairy-gift about them, as well as of the less poetical, but more substantial pleasure of a box from home at school'.[240] He had included twenty engravings, which delighted her and provided 'a gallery by the fireside'.

William's long delay in writing to Charlotte might also have been explained by a visit that he had made to Oxford after an interval of thirty years; he had last been there when he was twenty-one and still an apprentice, the year that Keats died. When put pen to paper, he must have written of the changes that had taken place. Reading further into the letter, it is not Oxford itself but a 'decaying hamlet'. As I suggested in the first chapter, we can perhaps take this to be Wheatley.

William had visited an old-maiden cousin who had

gossiped about his parents and had offered reminiscences of none but pleasant facts and characteristics.[241] Norman Penty explored William's family tree and I have tried to search further. The old-maiden cousin couldn't have been his great-aunt Susanna who, we saw earlier, had failed to include William in her will. The Ann Williams, who attended William's wedding was married and, by 1851, would almost certainly have died. William's father, Richard, did have a brother and a sister, who would have inherited under his will had William and his brother predeceased their parents. There was a child, but would that child, by 1851, have become 'old'? We don't know. I do take comfort in the reminiscences being none but pleasant.

Whilst on the subject of William's family, as noted before, the 1851 census shows that his eldest daughter, Margaret Ellen, was then a 'daily governess' and whilst her sister Fanny Emily was a teacher of music, and Mary Louisa was a scholar at Queen's College which she had entered at the age of sixteen to train as a teacher. It also tells that William Francis, the eldest son, was an Artist decorator, whilst Robert was a bookseller's clerk, Richard and Thornton were both scholars, and the youngest, Anna, a scholar at home. Letitia Mary Deacon was listed as a governess (we might presume for Anna) and, finally, there was Elizabeth Smith named as a general servant. All in what was really quite a small house. The later census reports, too, paint a picture of a household brimming with family members. Letitia Deacon's brother Harry (described elsewhere as a friend of William) would later teach Anna singing.

William observed that Oxford had changed. Charlotte writes of her anxiety that Cornhill might ever change. It is almost as if she can see storm clouds gathering, concerned that something she feared might alter what she had held precious. I think William's letter dwelt rather on the subject of friendship. Charlotte's response is to caution against misunderstanding how friendship works. She suggests that:

> In the matter of friendship I have observed that disappointment here arises chiefly – not from liking our friend too well – or thinking of them too highly – but rather from an over-estimate of their liking for and opinion of us; and that if we guard ourselves with sufficient scrupulousness of care from errors in this direction and can be content and even happy to give more affection than we receive and can make just comparison of circumstances and be sincerely accurate in drawing inferences thence, and never let self love blind our eyes – I think we may manage to get through life with consistency and constancy - unembittered by that misanthropy which springs form revulsions of feeling.[242]

She accepts that she may be sounding a little metaphysical, but ends with a pithy summary: 'We must love our friends for their sakes rather than for our own'.

In what must have been his next letter, William provided Charlotte with a vivid description of emigrants boarding a ship and this prompted Charlotte's reply of 26 September 1851. That year, the government was promoting emigration to Australia for men to farm the land deserted by those caught up in the Australian gold rush.[243] William had clearly pointed to the hardship that awaited the emigrants on the voyage and on their arrival, but also to the harsh conditions at home that prompted their decision to move. Charlotte presents a more positive view, highlighting the opportunities that a new country would offer, but first she makes an observation:

> As I laid down your letter after reading with interest the graphic account it gives of a very striking scene, I could not help feeling with renewed force a truth trite enough yet ever

impressive; viz; that it is good to be attracted out of ourselves to be forced to take a new view of the sufferings, the privations, the efforts, the difficulties of others.[244]

William seems also to have told Charlotte of the positive experience of his brother-in-law who had emigrated to Australia and was obviously having some success. The brother in law was Montague Ellis; he had married Margaret's youngest sister Sophia, and I have traced descendants living now in New Zealand. Good fortune has meant that some letters between the Hill siblings have survived and their descendent, Cheryl Pivac, has allowed me to use them and also family photographs. The nearest in date, and already referred to, is from Robert Hill to his sister and is from 1848.[245] The subject of emigration emerges again in a letter that Charlotte writes to Elizabeth Gaskell on 3 November, with a letter of introduction for William's son Frank (William Francis), 'a young artist now in Manchester'. William had written to Charlotte to ask if she would do this for him.

William's time was of course occupied by authors other than Charlotte Brontë. He had written to her about a new author, who, Margaret Smith suggests, might have been Miss Biggar with *The Fair Carew; or, Husbands and Wives*. Charlotte had read the book and, in her letter to William of 10 November, describes it as a 'delightful work of genuine metal, with a writer as shrewd as Miss Austen and not so shrewish'. She asks William to tell her whether the writer is young or middle-aged. We don't have his reply, but, in a subsequent letter to George Smith, she repeats her positive views on *Fair Carew*.

Holme Lee, the nom de plume for Mrs Parr, was another author highlighted in William's obituary in *The Publishers' Circular*. The *Dictionary of National Biography* - a Smith Elder & Co. publication - has a substantial entry on her. She was from Yorkshire. Her first novel, *Maude Talbot*, was published in 1854. It was her second, *Gilbert Massenger*, which brought her to public attention when she sent it to Charles Dickens who was 'much impressed and it was only its length that prevented it being published in *Household Words*'. Thereafter, she wrote a novel each year until her death in 1900, as well as more serious works including *The Life and Death of Jeanne D'Arc*.

Frank Williams comes to the fore in Charlotte's letter to William on the first day of the new year, with news of her poor health and associated difficulty in sitting at a desk, but also with an enquiry about his son, Frank: had he met with Mrs Gaskell? The answer to this question is to be found in her letter to Elizabeth Gaskell of 6 February 1852, where she expresses her pleasure at having read, in Elizabeth's letter, a report that 'young Mr Williams had impressed her agreeably'.[246] Full circle is reached in Charlotte's letter to William of a little over a year later (23 March 1853) when she writes:

> I lose no time in congratulating you on the favourable tidings received from your son. Both for his own sake and that of his parents – I earnestly hope Providence may prosper him in that new and remote region into which he has ventured; but I trust he will be careful, and be very sure of his own firm establishment before he holds out inducements to others to join him. He will naturally wish for solace of kindred affection, and perhaps may be tempted by that wish to overlook important difficulties. Will his kind father take care and not be too hasty on this point? A new career, a new sphere, a new clime offer temptations to sanguine minds; but let Prudence mingle her quiet word with whispers of Inclination.[247]

It may be that Frank did not take heed of this advice for, on 5 January 1855, he married Ellen Williams, then aged only fifteen.

The letters passing between William and Charlotte for a while contain the same felicitous tone, but have as their focus more down-to-earth matters: the next book. 1852 would be occupied with Charlotte's completion of the manuscript of *Villette* and a proposed second edition of *Shirley*. It would also mark a shift in correspondence with Charlotte writing more and more to Smith and Taylor. The first of these letters was about WM Thackeray's *Henry Esmond*.

For William, there is the letter of 25 March with which she returns her 'errata' of *Shirley,* which is about to move into its second edition. Whilst writing, she tells him of the pleasure she derived from reading The *Two Families: An Episode in the History of Chapelton* by Mrs Whitehead the author of *Rose Douglas*. She says that she also enjoyed Julia Kavanagh's *Women of Christianity,* but questions her understanding of Protestant ways. Religion is never far away from the Brontë-Williams correspondence.

The subject of the Cornhill book boxes continues in Charlotte's letter of 3 April. William had suggested that Charlotte should read *The School for Fathers: An Old English Story* by Talbot Gwynne (Josepha Galston). He had also asked her if she would write to him with her opinion of the novel. This seems to me to be another occasion when William had taken the role of teacher. In Charlotte's response, she says this: 'To speak candidly – I felt in reading the tale – a wondrous hollowness in the moral and sentiment; a strange dilettante shallowness in the purpose and feeling'.[248] As is so often the case, roles seem to reverse in the second half of the letter, when Charlotte challenges William's rather idealistic concept of the Model Man of Business, drawing his attention to human nature. Yet she returns, I think, to his views, when she writes: 'For how many is Life made a struggle – enjoyment and rest curtailed – labour terribly enhanced beyond almost what Nature can bear – I often think that this World would be the most terrible of enigmas were it not for the firm belief that there is a World to Come where conscientious effort and patient pain will meet their reward'.

Anna Williams was baptised at St James's Church, Westminster on 28 June 1852. This was some seven years after her birth. I have already noted my failure to find evidence that any of her siblings, other than the first five, had been baptised and I wonder a little at its significance. Was it, perhaps, that Anna herself wanted it? Could William have been swayed by Charlotte's comments?

By 1852, Charlotte's letters to William are becoming less frequent, with those to other correspondents growing: these include Elizabeth Gaskell, whom she is getting to know better, as well as admiring her writing (such as *Visiting at Cranford*). Charlotte's next letter to William is dated 28 July and contains a request to hold off publishing the second edition of *Shirley* until *Villette* is ready. She explains to William the causes of the delays in writing the latter. The first is her ill-health caused by the bitter winter and long, cold spring. The summer warmth has helped, but all is overshadowed by her father's illness. A further three months go by before, with a short note of 26 October, Charlotte forwards to William the first two volumes of *Villette*. She follows this up on 30 October with a letter to George Smith, seeking his 'honest thoughts'. Both George Smith and William read the manuscript of *Villette* and they both write to Charlotte with their comments. She replies to them individually. Her letter to William is dated 6 November 1852, and she clearly agrees with the points that he must have made about the plot. She doubts whether 'the regular novel reader will consider "the agony piled sufficiently high" – (as the Americans say) or the colours dashed on the Canvass with the proper amount of daring'.[249] William would surely have come to expect this type of reply and the fact that no changes would be made as a result.

I see *Villette* as quite different to both *Jane Eyre* and *Shirley*. In relation to any quest for evidence of William and the Cornhill parcels, the scene in the art gallery in Chapter 19 rather jumps out. I wonder what William would have made of it. I have to admit to finding part of it very funny, and so beg excuse at quoting a couple of sentences from it:

> These are not a whit like nature. Nature's daylight never had that colour; never was made so turbid, either by storm or cloud, as it is laid out there, under a sky of indigo: and that indigo is not ether; and those dark weeds plastered upon it are not trees.
>
> Several very well executed and complacent looking fat women struck me as by no means the goddesses they appeared to consider themselves.

The words are of course of the narrator, Lucy Snowe, but there are hints of the way Charlotte sometimes expresses strident views. In a fascinating paper entitled, '"These Are Not a Whit Like Nature": Lucy Snowe's Art Criticism in Villette', Emily Petermann explores Lucy's many observations on art.[250] I feel sure that William's efforts at art education might have helped Charlotte in writing these passages.

The book appears early in 1853 and is met by a large number of very warm reviews in the general press and also in the periodicals, such as *The Examiner* of 5 February 1853:

> This novel amply sustains the fame of the author of *Jane Eyre* and *Shirley* as an original and powerful writer. Though the plot is very slight and the whole work of it, if it had been one fourth shorter, might still have filled the orthodox three volumes, the pleasure it affords to the reader never flags. The men, women and children who figure throughout it have flesh and blood in them. All are worked out heartily, in such a way as to evince a very keen spirit of

observation on the author's part and a fine sense of the picturesque in character.

The Atlas of 12 February 1853 adds:

> Original and often grand in her delineation of character, dramatic to a high degree, powerful in the management of her plot with a strong sense of the meaning of Life and an earnest striving upwards and onwards, the authoress of Jane Eyre has secured a warm and hearty reception for Villette. The characters are developed with such minuteness of detail that any endeavour to place them before our readers by means of extracts would be as futile as an attempt to show the beauty and design of the rich oriel window by exhibiting a disconnected fragment of its tracery.

William, as before, sends to Charlotte the positive reviews, and she chastises him for not sending those that are less good. For example, she has heard that the *The Guardian* had reservations (mentioned in her letter of 7 March 1853). William then obviously forwards the adverse reviews post-haste, for she writes again on 9 March with her observations. 'Surely the poor Guardian Critic has a right to lisp his opinion that Currer Bell's female characters do not realise his notion of ladyhood – and even "respectfully decline" the honour of an acquaintance with "Jane Eyre" and "Lucy Snowe" without meriting on that account to be charged with having offered an "unmanly insult"'.[251]

In her letter of 29 March, Charlotte's chastising seems to come close to anger. She suggests that, however hard her publishers try to keep the harsh reviews from her, they will find a way through. She then adds that her publishers have indeed been wonderful in sending the good reviews, but, for the bad, she has had to rely on her friends. I have no way of knowing whether William ever 'talked shop' with his wife, but I feel sure that some words of exasperation would have slipped through his lips that evening. All his efforts in soothing her feelings on the few poor reviews of *Jane Eyre* and the rather more of *Shirley*. All forgotten.

Charlotte's letter to William of 8 April 1853 is remarkable in a number of ways. It deals with positive reviews of *Villette* - firstly those in Thornton Hunt's *Leader* magazine, which he had recently launched with George Lewes, and in *The Westminster* review. We might recall that, whilst Lewes loved *Jane Eyre*, he was less certain about *Shirley*.

Charlotte goes on to write the words that follow:

> My dear sir shall I tell you which is the cleverest of all the reviews and - inimical as it is - the one best calculated to give satisfaction to an author who can make up his mind wholly to dismiss personal vanity - and to disregard the persevering attempt at jarring his individual feelings?
>
> It is that in the Christian Remembrancer.
>
> Probably you have not read this review, or if you have glanced at it - you think the above declaration paradoxical. As I see the matter it appears thus. A clever hard headed high-church ecclesiastic of sinewy bigotry and genuine talent takes up a work of "Currer Bells" - detesting in his soul that same "Currer Bell" for his loose theological latitudinarianism, as well as for a tone of feeling and structure of thought utterly antipathetic to those owned by the stern, proud, able priest- his judge.
>
> The critic falls to work in better mood; he hates "Currer Bell" and if he can - he will grind the life out of him. He reads – cynically, contemptuously; he snarls, that he still reads. The book gets hold

of him, he curls his lip, he shows his teeth, he would fain anathematise; excommunicate the author; but he reads on, yes – and, as he reads - he is forced both to <u>feel</u> and to <u>like</u> some portion of what is driven into his hostile iron nature. Nor can he - in writing his critique altogether hide the involuntary partiality; he does his best; he still speaks big and harsh, trying to inflict on the author of personal pain, striking at hazard, guessing at weak points, but hoping always to hit home. And that author reads <u>him</u> with composure, lays down the review content and thankful - feeling that when an enemy is so influenced he has not written in vain.[252]

Following this quite remarkable passage, Charlotte acknowledges a more recent letter from William and, from what she writes, we can perhaps infer that he has laid bare his heart on a matter of personal concern. This time she does not comment or offer guidance, but merely wishes him to his best expectations a full realisation of that for which he longs. She ends by sending kind regards to Mrs Williams and her family.

On 28 May, Charlotte writes to thank William for a book box and then adds:

I have thought of you more than once during the late bright weather knowing how genial you find warmth and sunshine. I trust it has brought this season its usual cheering and beneficial effect. Remember me kindly to Mrs Williams and her daughters.[253]

On 6 December 1853, Charlotte wrote what is believed to be the last letter she addresses to William:

My dear Sir,

I forwarded last week a box of return books to Cornhill which – I trust arrived safely. To-day I received the "Edinburgh Guardian" for which I thank you.

Do not trouble yourself to select or send any more books. These courtesies must cease some day – and I would rather give them up than wear them out.

Believe me yours sincerely

C Brontë[254]

The explanation for this short harsh letter is to be found in her letter to George Smith of four days later, in which she offers her 'meed of congratulation'. Margaret Smith explains that this is of George's engagement. George Smith, himself, recalled this ungracious response which he compared to the congratulations he offered to Charlotte on her engagement (a year later) to Arthur Nichols. Margaret Smith suggests that Smith's engagement marked an end to Charlotte's personal relationship with her publisher.[255]

William is mentioned one more time, in Charlotte's letter to George Smith of 25 April 1854, in which she thanks Smith for his congratulations on her engagement. Of William she says, 'I sometimes wonder how Mr Williams is, and I hope he is well'. Her explanation follows: 'In the course of the year that is gone – Cornhill and London have receded a long way from me – the links of communication have waxed very frail and few'.[256] William, George and George's mother and sisters were, however, included in Charlotte's wedding cards. There is no record of whether any of them attended.

10 THE CORNHILL

William was blossoming in his role as Reader and de facto mentor to a good number of authors. It was his practice always to write a letter of criticism, even to those authors he rejected. However, there were more immediate matters to deal with.

Charlotte Brontë's death in 1855 surely sent shock waves through 65 Cornhill. It is not entirely straightforward to assess the accompanying emotions. William had opened his soul to Charlotte, but a year had passed since that final letter: time for both reflection and healing. He had kept her letters. He would have her manuscripts and copies of those reviews, both good and bad. He would also know that a good deal more writing could have come from Charlotte's pen.

George Smith had married. His business was progressing. He had lost one of his best authors on her marriage and possibly had given up all hope of her return. We do know that she was working on a new novel entitled *Emma*. However, Smith was above all a businessman and he was looking at ways to grow his list of authors. The creation of his brainchild, The *Cornhill Magazine,* was some years away, but ideas were beginning to take shape. An extract of *Emma* would appear in The *Cornhill* Magazine in an article with a sketch and words from Thackeray.[257]

The more immediate question of Charlotte Brontë took precedence. Following her death, a number of articles appeared that criticised Charlotte as a woman, rather than as an author. These caused hurt to Charlotte's friends, not least Elizabeth Gaskell. As a novelist, Gaskell was well regarded. Her most recent novel, *North and South,* had offered another sharp critique on British industrial society. She had received a letter of congratulation from Charles Dickens. Elizabeth decided that, for Charlotte, the record needed to be put straight, and she wrote to George Smith with the suggestion that she might write something. He concurred. The next hurdle was to convinced Charlotte's father and her husband of all too few months, Mr Nicholls. They, too, concurred, much to her surprise. Elizabeth set about her research, gathering such letters as correspondents would let her have. She obtained some three hundred letters from Charlotte's school friend Ellen Nussey and these gave her a sense of the parsonage and home life. She and Patrick Brontë exchanged a good number of letters.

Elizabeth needed to explore Charlotte Brontë the author, and so she wrote to William, seeking a loan of Charlottes letters to him. There were over a hundred letters covering the period of her life as a published author, spanning some seven years. There were those early ones, tentative and formal. There were then those that actually shed as much light on William as they did Charlotte. There were those where William was teaching her. There were those toward the end. William had kept them all. Smith Elder & Co. had a system under which an incoming letter would be placed in a small, pre-printed folder which would be marked with the date of receipt and the date when the reply was sent. However, we know that the letters were later passed down to William's son, Thornton, and so they must at some point have fallen outside the firm's systems.

Charlotte had told William that she had kept all of his letters and referred to them from time to time. The fact that only one of William's letters survived begs obvious questions. Did Charlotte destroy them when she, in effect, severed relationships with her publisher? Did Nicholls destroy them after her death? We don't know.

As to Charlotte's letters to William, he packaged them up and sent them to Elizabeth with a letter which referred also to the correspondence of some four years earlier concerning his son Frank's emigration to Australia. This is Elizabeth's reply

> Dear Sir,
>
> I am extremely obliged to you for the pacquet [sic] of Miss Brontë's letters which I found here on my return home, too late for Friday's post for me to acknowledge them. I have read them hastily over and I like the tone of them very much; it is curious how much the spirit in which she wrote varies according to the correspondent whom she was addressing, I imagine. I like the series of letters which you sent better than any other, excepting one I have seen. The subjects too are very interesting; how beautifully she speaks (for instance) of her wanderings on the moors after her sister's death. I am obliged to you, sir, for your kindness in sending them to me and I will take great care great care as long as they are in my keeping.
>
> I can fancy from the way in which you speak that your son's career in Australia has not been so prosperous as at one time both you and he hoped it might have been; but if you lived in such a town as this you will see how terribly injurious to young men mere worldly prosperity too often becomes. Still, Australia is a long way off, and his prolonged absence from you and his mother

must, I am sure, be a trial to both of you and him. Will you remember my meeting him when you write? Mr Gaskell thought he recognised him again in another Mr Williams we met at Chamounix this summer; he still thinks it might have been Frank Williams' brother to whom he spoke, the likeness was so great. Believe me to remain yours truly and obliged EC Gaskell[258]

Frank Williams had emigrated to New South Wales, and word coming back to England did not speak of the success he had hoped for. He had married Ellen in on 7 January 1855, and two children followed: Ellen in 1856 and Frank in 1857. Ellen shared the same surname as her husband and, as already noted, was possibly as young as fifteen when she married Frank. We can recall Charlotte's letter when she cautioned William on Frank encouraging others to follow him. There is more to say about Frank and Ellen in a later chapter.

There is a further point to make on the letters William sent; a number he held back. His daughter-in-law, Elizabeth Baumer Williams, wrote about these in *The Macmillan Magazine* of 1891. Thornton Williams married Elizabeth Baumer on 26 June 1866, and it was from this couple that Clement Shorter received the package of Charlotte's letters which he used for his book, *Charlotte Brontë and Her Circle* published in 1896. Elizabeth Baumer Williams wrote three articles for the Macmillan Magazine in June, July and August 1891, coincidentally the first three months of my father's (William's great-nephew's) life. She tells how, when Elizabeth Gaskell was writing Charlotte Brontë's biography, William kept back certain letters which, 'with scrupulous regard for the feelings of many people at that time living obliged Mr Williams to refuse them'. She goes on to say that Mrs Gaskell 'thoroughly appreciated his motives in withholding them'. Elizabeth Baumer Williams admitted to 'the good fortune [...] to posses a large number of these letters exchanged from time to time between distant friends; letters which are themselves a mine of wealth and beauty, and which are also interesting for their free and independent comment on the writers and topics of the day'. These are, therefore, not letters that reflect much on William and Charlotte's relationship, except for the frankness of her comments.

Elizabeth's article of June 1891 focuses on Charlotte's correspondence with William Makepeace Thackeray, to which I have already referred. Elizabeth quotes from a letter to William which makes really forthright comment. The letter is dated 11 December 1847:

> I hardly ever felt delight equal to that which cheered me when I received your letter containing an extract from a note by Mr Thackeray, in which he expressed himself gratified with the perusal of Jane Eyre. Mt Thackeray is a keen, ruthless satirist. I had never perused his writings but with feelings of blended admiration and indignation. Critics, it appears to me, do not know what an intellectual boa constrictor he is – they call him "humourous", "brilliant"; his is a most scalping humour, a most deadly brilliancy – he does not play with his prey, he coils round it and crushes it in his rings.

Charlotte sees Thackeray as taking a dim view of much of humankind, and Elizabeth sees Charlotte as doing something similar. William, as we have seen, for all his anxiety and self doubt, was inclined to a much more positive view.

Elizabeth's July article turns to William's friend George Lewes. I say William's friend, since there is much evidence of a close relationship. Frederick Wicks about whom I write later, though, cited Thackeray, Ruskin and Lewes's long-term partner, George Eliot as William's friends, so it would be wrong to attribute any motive of protection particularly to Lewes. Elizabeth's thesis on Lewes is that

Charlotte did not take exception to his criticism (although with *Shirley* she certainly seemed to as I have shown), but rather took great offence at Lewes's continual speculation about the gender of the writer. We might recall Thackeray's first letter to William where he is pretty clear in his assertion that Currer Bell was, indeed, a woman.

Elizabeth's August article begins by looking at letter writing, and is her lament that, by 1891, 'the influence of the postcard and telegram has so completely metamorphosed the spirit of our letter writing that it would need a keener insight than many of us could boast to read a man's nature through his letters'.[259] Charlotte had written to William in 1849 just that: "How easy it is to feel a man's nature through his letters! I felt something of your nature through the very first letter I received from you. I felt I might trust and need not fear. Through Mr Lewes's three or four epistles, his cast of disposition was discernable; the same might be said of Mr Taylor's correspondence.'

Enough, for now, of the letters which William did not send to Elizabeth Gaskell. She first met him in the middle part of 1856, when she was in full flow of the biography. In a letter to Ellen Nussey of 9 July 1856, she tells how 'Mr Williams dined there when I did; grey-haired, silent, and refined'.[260] The next mention of William comes in relation to the vexed subject of the posthumous publication of Charlotte's novel *The Professor*. Mrs Gaskell had run into problems when she went to Brussels to meet Monsieur and Madame Heger. They were most anxious that Charlotte's letters, referring to them and her love for Monsieur Heger, should not be published. Elizabeth concurred; her project was to 'make the world honour the woman as much as they have admired the writer'.[261] Pressure mounted for the publication of *The Professor*. Mr Nicholls released the manuscript to Elizabeth and she satisfied herself that there was no obvious reference to Heger which would cause problems: the manuscript did, however, need some revising prior to publication. Before this, she wrote to George Smith a letter which included the following passage, which makes particular reference to William:

> My own feeling as to any revision would be that Mr Williams should undertake it. I believe also from her opinions expressed in her letters - that he would be the person she would have chosen. She continually speaks of him in the highest terms - of his admirable taste in literature etc. - for my own part I think, as she had prepared it for the press, the editor should be careful and very scrupulous in making any alteration. Yours ever very truly EC Gaskell[262]

Juliet Barker tells that in the event it was Mr Nicholls who made the revisions.[263]

Another issue that Elizabeth Gaskell felt she must address was that of the unkind reviews. She obviously asked William to tell her of them. This was her response from October of 1856:

> I am very much obliged to you for your letter which gives me much of the information I wanted. How stupid of the reviewers not to find out its merit - cautious dancers. I had no idea they were so long about it. Yes, I should be very much obliged to you indeed if you would send me copies of the Athenaeum and Examiner notices. The Examiner is always a generous paper, if it does sometimes praise too much and too indiscriminately and from private personal motives. It never would let an unknown work of genius go without to a hearty good word, whoever was the author or the publisher and whatever newspapers had been niggardly in their dole. I suppose I may put in Mr Thackeray's little sentence about crying. It is far too good to be

lost. I beg your pardon for writing as untidily as I do (such a contrast to her neat delicate clear firm handwriting), but somehow I am always in a hurry. Yours very truly EC Gaskell[264]

Elizabeth sent sections of the draft biography to both William and George Smith to read, 'not as publishers but as Charlotte Brontë's friends'.[265] She also had long discussions with George Smith over the risk of libel. Smith's caution proved to be justified, and necessary adjustments were eventually made. Elizabeth Gaskell's *Life of Charlotte Brontë* was published in 1857. Smith Elder & Co. went on to publish her later works through the medium of *The Cornhill Magazine*, of which I write, at greater length, below.

Elizabeth Gaskell wrote to him on 20 December 1860, enclosing a manuscript from a Miss Burnett, whom she had met on holiday. She explained that she had sent it straight to him because she had sent rather a lot to Mr Smith, adding 'besides you have always been so kind to me, however and whenever I have applied to you, that I think you would forgive me, if my bringing this [manuscript] under your notice should uselessly waste your time.'[266] In the same letter, she says how much she enjoyed seeing Lowes Dickinson on the previous Saturday and how, on a recent visit to Haworth, she found the elderly Mr Brontë much weakened and Mr Nicholls ever more unpopular.

In or around 1855, William and Margaret had moved to 6 Sussex Place, Canonbury, Islington and it was from there that on 5 June 1855 that Fanny Emily married journalist and author William James Sorrell. They married at Islington Parish Church. William Smith Williams occupation is listed on her marriage certificate as a publisher. There were two witnesses recorded, J. M. Langford and J. Deacon. Langford was an author who worked with Sorrell. The mention of the name Deacon, once again indicates a relationship between the Williams and Deacons. Letters written by Margaret Williams to her sister Sophia Louisa Ellis (née Hill), who was living in New Zealand, reveal that Fanny's marriage didn't last very long; 'Sorrell went off with an actress soon after they were married'.[267] Having said this, the 1861 census shows Fanny living with her husband and his father (a commercial traveller), his mother and Fanny's sister Anna. A break of two years followed and, on 15 July 1857, Mary Louisa ('Tiny') married Alexander Robertson at St Stephen's Church Islington.

Just a few months later on 15 October 1857, at All Souls Church, Langham Place, Marylebone, Ellen married William's friend and colleague of many years, Cato Lowes Dickinson. This latter wedding might well have achieved some celebrity since the Morning Post of 17 October reports that the Officiant was F.D. Maurice, the well-known Christian socialist and founder of the Working Men's College, where, of course, he worked with Lowes Dickinson. It is surely likely that in addition to family, there would have been friends among the wedding guests: Ford Madox Brown, William Rossetti (and quite probably Dante Gabriel and Christina), and John Ruskin.

William's liberal outlook and that of his family and circle, combined with the location, makes it entirely possible that there was a link to one of the first women's suffrage groups: The Langham Place Group.[268] As already noted, Harriet Martineau was a signatory in the 1866 petition to Parliament on women's suffrage.

Grandchildren soon followed. Lowes Dickinson and Ellen, who were living in Langham Chambers, Marylebone, had Arthur on 8 August 1859, Margaret in 1861 and Goldsworthy on 6 August 1862. By the time Hester was born in 1865, the family had moved to Spring Cottage, in the village of Hanwell, set in 'beautiful and picturesque scenery', some eight miles west of Paddington. Janet followed in 1866.

Happiness was to be short-lived for, on 16 January

1861, William's still recent son-in-law, Alexander Robertson, died leaving a widow, Mary Louisa, and two small children Alice and Louis. The 1861 census records that they went to live with William and Margaret, by which time they had moved to 16 Claremont Row, Islington. Also in the household were Robert (then a banker's clerk), Richard (a commercial clerk), and granddaughter Ellen Margaret Williams (aged four and recorded as having been born in New South Wales). The presence of this little granddaughter brings William's eldest son back into the story, although rather shrouded in mystery. Frank had married the very young Ellen and they had had two children, Ellen and Frank. The records show that both children were baptised in St Mary's Church in Islington on 28 August 1859. Both parents were present, and father Frank was recorded as an artist. I am indebted to Dr Christine Hutchison and Fran Manning for their research into this Australian branch of William's family and I return to this in the next chapter.

We now come to the story of *The Cornhill*. The success of Dickens's periodical, *All the Year Round*, was well known; in 1859, he published *A Tale of Two Cities* recalling the events of the Second French Revolution. Over the previous twenty years, his novels had been greatly aided by his practice of publishing them in instalments. George Smith had long been pondering following suit. He had had in mind a daily sheet of general criticism covering literature as well as general affairs. He and Thackeray had come up with *Fair Play* as a possible name. The idea never reached publication largely, Huxley suggests, because 'Thackeray shrank from the responsibilities of editorship'.[269] It did, however, find a place in Smith Elder & Co.'s Indian business in the form of *The Overland Mail*. Eventually, it assumed the form of a British periodical entitled *The Cornhill Magazine*, after Smith Elder & Co.'s address.

In 1860, George Smith appointed W.M. Thackeray as editor of his new *Cornhill Magazine*.: this was a master stroke. *The Cornhill* not only boasted, in its first editions, *Lovel the Widower* by Thackeray but also, and perhaps more importantly, Trollope's *Framley Parsonage*. It was probably the combination of these two very well-known authors that attracted an initial circulation of 110,000, which Jenifer Glynn compares to that of the Macmillan's Magazine of 10,000–15,000, which had been started by the much bigger publishing house of the same name in late 1859.[270] Huxley writes how Thackeray was justly proud of his success as editor:

> The enormous circulation achieved by the Cornhill Magazine when it was first started with Thackeray for its editor in chief is a matter of literary history. The announcement by his publishers that a sale of a hundred and ten thousand of the first number had been reached made the editor half delirious with joy and he ran away to Paris to be rid of the excitement for a few days. I met him by appointment at his hotel in the Rue de la Paix and found him wild with exultation and full of enthusiasm for excellent George Smith his publisher. London he exclaimed is not big enough to contain me now and I am obliged to add Paris to my residence.[271]

The *Cornhill*, largely through the efforts of George Smith, attracted renowned authors such as Wilkie Collins with *Armadale*. Later, it would attract Thomas Hardy and Henry James. In due course, George Smith would add *The Pall Mall* magazine to his publishing ventures. William had been busy, both with his daily work of reading submissions, but also with *The Cornhill*, where Thackeray would frequently refer submissions to him.

William's involvement with *The Cornhill* is clear from correspondence addressed to Thackeray as editor and passed to William to deal with. I explored the Smith Elder & Co. archive, which is held at the National Library of

Scotland, and found many files containing correspondence with authors, many with the pre-printed letter folder already described. The files for Thackeray and Trollope contain only correspondence with George Smith. Thackeray's does also have some of his original illustrations for *Philip,* which are a delight. There is also a draft of *Denis Duval,* his unfinished final novel. No mention of William. The same is true of correspondence with illustrators. George Smith writes to John Everett Millais about illustrating *Framley Parsonage.* He also writes to Frederick Walker, a talented young artist who illustrated an edition of *Jane Eyre.*

It wasn't just George Smith who was writing to the celebrated artists of the day. William, of course, knew many of them. Below is a letter to William from Christina Rossetti, dated 24 February 1860. He had met him at Mr G. Epps and took the opportunity to forward to him a piece by her brother, William Rossetti. Some seven years later there are letters, now, from William Rossetti offering pieces to *The Cornhill* from his friend Mr Stillman; those letters were not designated to be handled by William.

This though was not the case with three letters from Dante Gabriel Rossetti. These were all personal to WS Williams, and two concerned his book *Early Italian Poets.* The first seeks William's confidential help in enabling Rossetti to repay a debt to John Ruskin. The second has William sending an account of monies due. The third continues reference to Italian poets, but adds this:

> Since our "Joseph" correspondence, it had occurred to me whether its author may be lately dead. Is it so? I should regret to hear that yet another man of genius has failed recognition in his lifetime.[272]

Watts Dunton also picks up on this further attempt at the publication of Charles Wells's poem. He explains how Rossetti managed to resurrect Swinburne's rejected article, adding further extracts of the poem and had it published in *The Fortnightly Review*. He adds that William, and indeed George Meredith, made further efforts to find a publisher, but to no avail.[273] As I tell later, William was to have one last, and successful, attempt at finding a publisher to place Wells's poem on the literary stage.

Thackeray stepped down as editor of *The Cornhill* in 1862 and George Smith moved into the editor's chair, but, importantly, with George Lewes as editorial adviser. Thackeray died in December 1863 and George Lewes recorded in his journal his memory of the burial in Kensal Green Cemetery. 'There was a very large gathering between a thousand and 1500 people, among them most of the literary and artistic celebrities'.[274]

George Smith, with help from George Lewes, persuaded George Eliot to publish her next novel, *Romola*, in *The Cornhill*. She was offered a handsome fee which greatly exceeded anything her usual publisher, Blackwood, could pay. Blackwood was upset, but resigned. Smith was delighted and sent gifts to her. He had persuaded Frederick Leighton to illustrate the novel in *The Cornhill* and he sent to Eliot a set of mounted photographs of the woodblock drawings. He also sent her a copy of DG Rossetti's *The Early Italian Poets*, which Smith Elder & Co. had published in 1861.[275] Haight tells that *Romola* was not the success that Smith had hoped, and that Smith turned down the manuscript of *Felix Holt* when George Lewes sent it to him.[276] In his refusal letter, he explained that he had read it to his wife and they thought it would be insufficiently commercial. There is no note of William's opinion or indeed of him having read it. George Lewes sent it to Eliot's original publishers, Blackwood, who quickly paid £5,000. *Felix Holt* remains one of Eliot's least-known novels and, indeed, was not a great commercial success. Lewes though had kept his connection with Smith Elder & Co. through their new title *The Pall Mall*, the first number of which appeared on 7 February 1865. It was only a few years later that Lewes sent *Middlemarch* directly to Blackwood, presumably with no thought for Smith Elder & Co. William was then in his seventies, but still working. George Eliot shared with William a high regard for and strong appreciation of painting. Like William, she had found inspiration in John Ruskin's writing.[277]

Nathaniel Hawthorne is best known as the author of *The Scarlet Letter*, said to have been the first piece of American literature to win the worlds approval as a classic, yet he once described himself as 'the obscurest man of letters in America'. He was a quiet man with a 'dark, introspective vision' which had about it, as his friend Herman Melville remarked, a 'great power of blackness deriving from a Calvinistic sense of Innate Depravity and Original Sin'.[278] In 1853, Hawthorne was appointed United States Consul in Liverpool, second in dignity to the Ambassador. He returned to America in 1857, but, in 1860, visited Leamington Spa. It was from there that he carried on a correspondence with William about a book entitled *The Marble Faun: Or, The Romance of Monte Beni*. The correspondence is cordial, but focuses on the process of publication. At one point Hawthorne asks William whether he considers the title suited to the British market. The book was about a fantastical Italy, and the result of the correspondence was to issue it in Britain under the title *Transformation*. William sent copies to Mr Chorley at *The Athenaeum* and to other reviewers.

In 1860 correspondence from Wilkie Collins was directed to William. *The Woman in White* had been published in *All the Year Round* and Smith, Elder & Co. were approached about printing a book edition. No transaction resulted, since Collins wished to retain the copyright. Collins later contributed to *The Cornhill Magazine*. Smith, Elder & Co. also issued various one volume editions: *Armadale* and, in 1871, *The Moonstone*. Correspondence with George Meredith from 1864 was directed to William's desk. It dealt with the pricing and sale of copyright in *Farina*. Later correspondence was directed not to William, but to his colleagues, to deal first with further copyrights, but then, in 1869, with the publication of his novel *Harry Richmond*. William returned to the correspondence on 31 October 1871 with a personal request to forward a copy of *Harry Richmond* to his friend Lionel Robinson.

Some eighteen months after Alexander's death, the Williams family's spirits would have been lifted by the marriage, on 8 August 1863, of Robert Henry to Emily Epps. Emily was the second daughter of George Napoleon Epps, whom the Williams had known for some years. I searched for some information about their marriage and found a reference to a picture, *The Wedding of St George*, by Dante Gabriel Rossetti: Robert had given it to Emily on the occasion of their wedding, and Emily had bequeathed it to Ellen ('Nellie') Gosse, her sister, on her death in 1912.[279] Robert was a talented amateur artist and Emily, although less well known than her sister, produced some acclaimed work. The newly married couple lived in New Cavendish Street and Robert earned his living as a bank manager. Emily's sister Ellen had married Edmund Gosse and she did indeed have a celebrated career as a painter.

Tragedy struck, again, on 17 October 1864 when Robert was found dead in his house. The proceedings at the Coroners for Central Middlesex were reported in a number of newspapers including the *Usk Observer and Monmouth Central Advertiser* on 29 October 1864, William, whose address was given as 13 Ampthill Square, had been called upon to identify his son's body. He gave evidence that he had last seen Robert alive the previous Sunday when he found him in his usual health, but much depressed in spirits, and harassed about bank affairs. He had heard of his death on the Tuesday morning. The post-mortem had revealed death by cyanide of potassium. Robert's brother confirmed that he was a photographer, and so we can infer that he had access to such chemicals. It was Robert's father-in-law, George Epps, (who met with him frequently) that Robert had gone to see on that Monday evening. Epps had been out and Robert had returned and asked his manservant, Drake, for a brandy whilst he ran himself a bath. At five to ten Robert asked Drake to fetch Epps, but when Epps returned Robert was already dead. His wife, Emily, had been out at the theatre with a brother-in-law who was visiting town.

On 20 October, Emily purchased a grave plot in Kensal Green Cemetery and Robert was buried on 22 October 1864. Emily did not remarry, and she lived until 1912. She had been a promising artist but hardly painted after her husband's death. Robert's sister, Anna, gave an interview on her retirement, and the interviewer noted that in her house 'there is a large crayon sketch of Leigh Hunt hanging on the dining room wall, the work of one brother (Robert), who would have been an exceptionally clever artist had he lived (he was only a lad at the time he sketched this); while in the drawing room was an exquisite portrait of a great-grand-daughter of the poet'.

One particular theme emerges strongly in the archived letters: the immense care that William took of his authors, whether accepted for publication or not.

Elizabeth Gaskell wrote to William, in 1862, to seek his guidance for herself. We can infer that she had been struggling with her novel *Sylvia's Lovers*.

> My dear sir
>
> You must please consider this letter as private for I want to consult you about one or two things. In the first place have you read my two vols of my new novel? If you have, I'm afraid you do not like them because you say nothing about them. If you have, I should like to send you a sketch of the third vol to make you see how everything in the first two works up to the events and crisis in

that. If you have not read it, I should be very glad if you would tell me, as I cannot help feeling a little disheartened by the ambiguous sentence in your note today, which I cannot interpret either one way or another as to your having read it or not. If somebody (out of my family) would be truly interested in my poor story, it would give me just the fillip of encouragement I want. I am sure you will understand this feeling, though you may think I ought to be too strong to have it. Mr Smith who had it (the manuscript of the first two vols) for a month has never said a word about it; which has made me fear he does not like it, and though I do not imagine him to be any great judge of it from an artistic point of view, yet as our bargain was made beforehand I should be so sorry if he felt himself bound to take it whether he liked it or no. I cannot help liking it myself, but that may be because firstly I have taken great pains with it and secondly I know the end; and I cannot help thinking that if you have read it, and didn't like it at present, you will when it is finished and you see how it all works up to the crisis. But then authors are so easily deceived about their own things. Mind, I don't want you to read it only to tell me whether you have or not.

The letter goes on to ask about Julia Kavanagh's book and how far it may overlap the subject matter of her own other proposed work, *Madame de Sévigné*. Elizabeth had been asked to contribute to Dickens's periodical *All the Year Round,* but she expressed her reluctance to publish *Sylvia* in this way. Her letter continues:

Now may I ask how far this ground has been preoccupied by Ms Kavanagh or how far, supposing it had not been occupied by her, do you think Mr Smith would care to publish such a one volume work? Do not tell him if you please, as it would be a pain to me to have him troubled about a thing he may reject. And I should only regard your opinion as an opinion and not as the verdict. If I sent it to *All the Year Round,* they would publish it in bits I know and I think that publishers Chapman and Hall would take it afterwards. But I should not like to publish anything with any other publisher than Mr Smith till my novel was completed, unless now it came to pass. I hope you understand this rather confused letter and will allow me to consult you as a friend on all these points. I'm sure you will consider this letter confidential and believe me to remain dear sir, yours ever most truly, EC Gaskell.[280]

Winifred Gérin tells how, following this letter, Elizabeth's life was challenged by misfortune. The book, though, was eventually finished, with the third volume falling short in quality of the first two, with the result that the reviews were poor. Having said this, there is a letter from George Eliot to George Smith in which she says, 'Sylvia's Lovers seems to me of a high quality in both feeling and execution'.[281] Notwithstanding any problems over *Sylvia,* a good working relationship had grown between Elizabeth, William and George Smith, and she would become one of his core authors and so very much part of his plan to grow the business. *Cousin Phyllis* and *Wives and Daughters* were published by Smith Elder & Co.

In 1867, RD Blackmore had corresponded with one of William's colleagues about how to improve the manuscript of *Lorna Doone.* Revisions were made and a manuscript arrived in the spring of 1868 and was placed on William's desk. He must have written a kind and positive letter of rejection, for Blackmore replied on 30 May in the most cordial of terms. Blackmore, too, later contributed to *The Cornhill.* Some years later Huxley noted that 'it was the literary policy of the firm to continue Smith Williams's practice of writing a letter of criticism to the author of a rejected manuscript'.[282] He added, 'Smith, Elder received a very large number of grateful letters from young writers, who, however dashed by the rejection, were enabled to realise the care and sympathy meted out to their work, and ultimately profited from their criticisms'.

George Manville Fenn was a prolific novelist and, in the Smith, Elder correspondence, there are several of letters, one of which tells a story similar to those experienced by a good number whose manuscripts landed on William's desk. His letter of 3 May 1866 begins with these words:

> You gave me, if I may make use of the term, so kind and courteous a refusal of the last work I sent for your inspection, that I venture to ask your consent for the consideration of another.[283]

He goes on to explain that the book will be similar to his sketches published in *All the Year Round* on struggles in humble life and it would have the title 'A Struggle for the Crust'. No such title appears among Fenn's published works. Other titles do appear; Fenn becomes editor of Cassell's Magazine and, using their letterhead, writes to William on 20 February 1871, seeking to offer his next title. It is reasonable to suppose that he did, for on 7 November 1871 he writes, '[manuscript] safely received. Better luck next time perhaps'.

These letters give a sense of the work being done by William and also a sense of him. This was strongly the case with Frederick Wicks, a writer of the late nineteenth century ,whose works include a textbook on the British Constitution, which went into many editions, and novels including *Golden Lives: The Story of a Woman's Courage,* the introduction to which perhaps offers evidence that the advice William gave him had been taken.[284] The volume has a great number of illustrations, which, Wicks explains, are there to save the reader long paragraphs of description, leaving the words to carry the plot.

In an interview, given to *The Realm Magazine*, Wicks offers rather a unique picture of William. He begins by quoting Mrs Oliphant telling how 'the manuscript of Jane Eyre had travelled round all the publishing houses, probably unread in most of them, until Mr Williams attacked the terrible calligraphy and discovered a genius. His industry and patience were amazing; and as a counsellor he was untiring'.

Wicks tells how he encountered William when Thackeray was editing *The Cornhill*. He had submitted a manuscript which Thackeray had passed to William. Wicks goes on to sat that, 'the manuscript was not accepted but I shall always remember with extreme satisfaction the repeated efforts made by Mr Williams, by letter and in conversation, to induce me to abandon an ill-paid occupation and devote myself to fiction'. I can't help wondering whether, in Wicks, William saw his younger self.

Wicks continues, 'On the walls of his little room in the great publishing house on Cornhill were portraits of Thackeray, Ruskin, and George Eliot'. He talks of William's 'graceful manner, his winning smile, his uniform and almost unexampled courtesy, and of how he 'illustrated his arguments on literary style, construction and the cause of popularity by reference to the dicta and example of these his friends, the great novelists of the nineteenth century'. Wicks says that William 'discussed them all – laid bare their failings and lauded their merits – with a zest never to be forgotten'.

Wicks's description of William surely brings him to life:

> Thrusting back his massive growth of white hair, he would clasp his hands nervously in thought before delivering his opinion, and then would follow in short, pregnant sentences a perfect flood of light upon the matter in hand. He was

never content with general commendation and approval, but always gave good, sound reasons and sufficient cause for all he thought. Among the many pregnant phrases that fell to my lot was one of extraordinary value as a check to the exuberance of youth. "You need," he says,' "restraint – not that which checks, but that which guides the literary faculty".

Wicks adds that 'Mr Williams throughout his discourse exhibited a decided preference for the dramatic as opposed to the merely descriptive narrative'.[285]

It might have been that William was rejecting too much light literature and that encouraged George Smith to opt for someone quite different as his successor. That comes later in the story, for now my research into the John Ruskin folder at the National Library of Scotland revealed that William had other fish to fry.

11 RUSKIN YEARS

William's seventh decade could easily have been a gentle slowing down of his rate of work towards a well-earned retirement. Fate had something else in store.

John Ruskin had been published by Smith, Elder & Co. from the start, and his letters indicate that, following the death of his cousin Charles Richardson, Mr Harrison had then dealt with his day-to-day publishing concerns. Volumes 2 and 3 of *The Stones of Venice* had appeared in 1853, with Volumes 3 and 4 of *Modern Painters* following in 1856. George Smith, in his memoir, writes of some of Ruskin's other Smith, Elder & Co. publications: *The King of the Golden River*, *Notes on the Construction of Sheepfolds* and *Pre-Raphaelitism*. Each year he would write *Notes on the Royal Academy*.

I write this in the year of the bicentenary of John Ruskin's birth, and this has been marked in many ways, not least in the publication of two new books on Ruskin: *Ruskinland: How John Ruskin Shapes Our World* by Andrew Hill and *To See Clearly: Why Ruskin Matters*, by Suzanne Fagence Cooper. Both books take as their text the relevance of the writings of John Ruskin in today's world. No useful purpose would be served by my repeating the points they make, but I would highlight just two. Cooper places emphasis on Ruskin's belief in seeing the world around us. One particular sight is chilling since, one hundred and fifty years ago, Ruskin saw how polluted air was destroying the planet.[286] Hill looks at Ruskin's legacy and tells how Clement Atlee was inspired by Ruskin's writings on Political Economy.[287]

My aim is to shed a little light on how Ruskin worked with his publishers, but also the relationship that developed between him and William.

George Smith played a key part in the relationship as Ruskin's letter of May 1855 bears evidence:

Dear Mr Smith,

I believe Spottiswoode must have kept some of their men home to finish this. I am very much obliged to them, and should like the printers who stayed in to do it to have half a crown each, from me, for a holiday present. Will you kindly give orders to that effect? The proofs now sent back must be carefully revised by the press corrector - but I don't want to see another revise: so the moment they are ready, let the thing be printed off, and sold forthwith as near the doors of the Academy as may be.

Please send a copy of the pamphlet, the moment you have any ready, to Mr JF Lewis, Mr G Richmond, Miss AF Mutrie, Mr DG Rossetti (14 Chatham Place, Blackfriars Bridge) Mr William Rossetti, same address; Miss Heaton, 16 Beaumont Street Cavendish Square; Dr Acland, Oxford; and Mr Harrison; - all with my compliments.

Send to nobody else - of course Mr Williams will have one.

I send to town that all may be ready for early

press tomorrow morning.

Most truly yours, J Ruskin[288]

The pamphlet referred to in Ruskin's letter was the first of his series of *Royal Academy Notes*. This was followed by *Elements of Drawing, Political Economy of Art, Notes on Turner's Pictures, The Two Paths,* and *Elements of Perspective*.[289]

The relationship was clearly a close one. Huxley relates the story of the Nelson Sherry. James Ruskin, John's father, was a partner in the British firm importing Domecq sherry. 'Shortly before the Battle of Trafalgar, Nelson sent an order to Mr Ruskin's firm for some sherry. They sent him the finest they had; then, on sentimental grounds, the partners decided that not another glass from that particular butt should be sold. Each member of the firm, however, was allowed his portion, paying for it at the price at which it stood in the firm's ledger'.[290] George Smith would be honoured by the offering of Nelson Sherry.

The involvement of William with Ruskin is also evidenced by this letter of 4 August 1856 from James Ruskin to William:

My dear Sir,

I hear that in the Athenaeum of 26 July there is a good article on my son's Harbours of England and I should be greatly obliged by Mr Gordon [sic] Smith sending me that number.

The history of this book, I believe, I told you. Gambart, the French publisher and picture dealer, said some eighteen months ago that he was going to put out twelve Turner plates, never published, of English Harbours, and he would give my son two good Turner drawings for a few pages of text to illustrate them. John agreed, and wrote the text when poorly in the spring of 1855, at Tunbridge Wells; and it seems the work has just come out. It was in my opinion an extremely well done thing, and more likely, as far as it went, if not to be extremely popular, at least to be received without cavil than anything he had written. If there is a very favourable review in the Athenaeum...it may tend to disarm the critics, and partly influence opinion of his larger works....- With our united kind regards, John James Ruskin[291]

On 1 July 1860, John Ruskin sent to William, for *The Cornhill*, the first of his essays on Political Economy. He wrote:

Dear Mr Williams,

I send you some Political Economy, which, if you can venture to use in any way for the Cornhill, stigmatizing it by any notes of reprobation which you may think necessary, I shall be very glad. All I care about is to get it into print, somehow. Please, if you use it, put it on slips, and send it to me to Hotel de l'Universe, Chamonix, Faucigny, France. I shall send it back by the next post but one, and shall not need another revise. Send proof of slips also to my father.

I'm afraid you have had a great deal of trouble about that book of mine. I wish the binders had had a little more - but things must be as they may. I am very glad to be at last 'unbound' myself, so perhaps the book will be.

Kindest regards to Mr Smith. Ever faithfully and affectionately yours, J Ruskin.[292]

His *Political Economy* did indeed cause a stir. Elizabeth Smith suggests that it triggered a breakdown in the cordial relationship previously enjoyed with Ruskin by George Smith. The reason was that Smith was concerned was that his readership might be offended by Ruskin's socialist ideas. Four instalments of what became Ruskin's *Unto This Last* appeared between July and December 1860. In them, Ruskin is at pains to remove the setting of a man's wages for the work he does from the forces of supply and demand. He asserts that an hour of work has a value which remains the same irrespective of how many are offering the work and how many are needed. He suggests that a system of payment akin to that operated by the army would be superior to that in use in the world of manufacturing. He offers many examples and, in the fourth piece, attempts to set out some definitions. He starts, though, with an underlying principle: 'Just payment of labour consists in a sum of money which would approximately obtain equivalent labour at a future time'.[293]

For William, I think, this breakdown had a double silver lining for it not resulted in him leading the Smith, Elder & Co. relationship with John Ruskin, really until he retired and Ruskin took his publishing elsewhere, but it also, surely, gelled with his own views.

The first manifestation of this new relationship was the publication of William's *Selections from the Writings of John Ruskin*. In the Ruskin archive at the University of Lancaster, there is a first edition of the *Selections*. Of all the papers connected with William which I have viewed or touched, this meant the most. It is said to have been the last piece of work that William 'wrote', albeit as editor. It is clear to me that William had, all his life, longed for recognition as a writer and such recognition never came. His genius was in reading, but, as is so often the case, that didn't seem to satisfy his ambition. His reading of Ruskin's writings over a number of decades had won for him a remarkable appreciation, as is evidenced in the *Selections*. Sadly, I own only a later edition by Ruskin's later publisher George Allen, of whom there is more below. In William's first edition, the reader is served an eclectic selection of delights. They are taken from Ruskin's published works: *Modern Painters, The Seven Lamps of Architecture, The Stones of*

CHARLOTTE BRONTË'S DEVOTEE

Venice, Lectures on Architecture and Painting, The Two Paths, The Harbours of England, The Political Economy of Art. The introduction is from *Modern Painters*:

> In these books of mine, their distinctive character, as essays on art, is there bringing everything to a root in human passion or human hope. Arising first not in any desire to explain the principles of art, but in the endeavour to defend an individual painter from injustice, they have been coloured throughout -nay continually altered in shape, and even warped and broken, by digressions respecting social questions, which had for me an interest tenfold greater than the work I had been forced into undertaking. Every principle of painting which I have stated is traced to some vital or spiritual fact; and in my works on architecture the preference accorded finally to one school over another is founded on comparison of their influences on the life of the workmen - a question by all other writers on the subject of architecture only forgotten or despised. [294]

William chose this passage from among very many. In much of his dialogue with Charlotte Brontë, there is the theme of being rooted in truth. The reference to the influence of architecture on the life of the workman surely finds an echo in Ruskin's endeavours with the Working Men's College, with which William strongly sympathised. The volume is divided into themed sections: Scenes of Travel, Characteristics of Nature, Painting and Painters, Architecture and Sculpture, Ethical and Miscellaneous and it runs to some four hundred pages. Some brief extracts may help to give a flavour:

> **Painting a language:** Painting, or art generally, as such, with all its technicalities, difficulties, and particular ends, is nothing but a noble and expressive language, invaluable as the vehicle of

thought, but by itself nothing. He who has learned what is commonly considered the whole heart of painting, that is, the art of representing any natural object faithfully, has as yet only learnt the language by which his thoughts are to be expressed.[295]

Pre-Raphaelitism: Pre-Raphaelitism has but one principle, that of absolute uncompromising truth and all that it does, obtained by working everything, down to the most minute detail, from nature, and from nature only. Every Pre-Raphaelite landscape background is painted to the last touch, in the open air, from the thing itself. Every Pre-Raphaelite figure, however studied in expression, is a true portrait of some living person. Every minute accessory is painted in the same manner [...] This is the main Pre-Raphaelite principle. (Architecture and Painting Lecture 4)[296]

Architecture distinguished from building: Architecture is the art which so disposes and adorns the edifices raised by man, for whatever uses, that the sight of them may contribute to his mental health, power, and pleasure.

It is very necessary at the outset of all enquiry, to distinguish carefully between Architecture and Building.

To build - literally, to confirm – is by common understanding to put together and adjust the several pieces of any edifice or receptacle of a considerable size. Thus we have church building, house building, ship building and coach building. That one edifice stands, another floats, and another is suspended on iron springs, makes no difference in the nature of the art, if so it may be called, of building or edification. The persons who profess that art, are severally builders, ecclesiastical, naval, or of whatever other name their work may justify; but building does not become architecture merely by the stability of what it erects; and it is no more architecture which raises a church, or which fits it to receive and contain with comfort a required number of persons occupied in certain religious offices, than it is architecture which makes the carriage commodious or ship swift.[297]

The Slave Ship: I think, the noblest sea that Turner has ever painted, and, if so, the noblest certainly ever painted by man, is that of the Slave Ship, the chief Academy picture of the Exhibition of 1840. It is a sunset on the Atlantic, after a prolonged storm; but the storm is partially lulled, and the torn and steaming rain-clouds are moving in scarlet lines to lose themselves in the hollow of the night. The whole surface of sea included in the picture is divided into two ridges of the whole ocean, like the lifting of its bosom by deep drawn breath after the torture of the storm. Between these two ridges the fire of the sunset falls along the trough of the sea, dyeing it with an awful but glorious light, the intense and lurid splendour which burns like gold, and bathes like blood.[298]

Decay of Venice: The decay of the city of Venice is, in many respects, like that of an outwearied and aged human frame; the cause of its decrepitude is indeed at the heart, but the outward appearances of it are first that the extremities. In the centre of the city there are still places where some evidence of vitality remains, and where, with kind closing of the eyes to signs, too manifest even there, of distress and declining fortune, the stranger may succeed in imagining, for a little while, what must have been the aspect of Venice in her prime. But this lingering pulsation has not force enough any more to penetrate into the suburbs and outskirts of the city; the frost of death has there seized upon it irrevocably, and the grasp of mortal disease is marked daily by the increasing breath of its belt of ruin.

Mental slavery of modern workmen: Reader, look around this English room of yours, about which you have been proud so often, because the work of it was so good and strong, and the ornaments of it so finished. Examine again all those accurate mouldings and perfect polishings, and unerring adjustments of the seasoned wood and tempered steel. Many a time you have exulted over them, and thought how great England was, because her slightest work was done so thoroughly. Alas! if read rightly, these perfectnesses are signs of a slavery in our England a thousand times more bitter and more degrading than that of the scourged African or helot Greek. Men may be beaten, chained, tormented, yoked like cattle, slaughtered like summer flies, and yet remain in one sense, in the best sense, free. But to smother their souls within them, to blight and hew into rotting pollards the suckling branches of their human intelligence, to make the flesh and skin which, after the worm's work on it, is to see God, into leathern thongs to yoke machinery with - this it is to be slave masters indeed;

Ruskin finishes this piece, which extends over three pages, with what he identifies as three simple and broad rules:

Never encourage the manufacture of any article

not absolutely necessary, in the production of which *Invention* has no share.

Never demand an exact finish for its own sake, but only for some practical or noble end.

Never encourage imitation or copying of any kind, except for the sake of preserving record of great works.

Ruskin's concern was that the invention of craftsmen was at risk from the regimentation of manufacture. He said of Lincoln Cathedral:

> I have always held (and am prepared against all comers to maintain my holding) that the Cathedral of Lincoln is out and out the most precious piece of architecture in the British islands, and—roughly—worth any two other cathedrals we have got.[299]

Ruskin would have loved the lack of uniformity of the lines of its roof. The letter from which this was taken has further observations that are typical of Ruskin. The letter was addressed to WT Page, who was the then Mayor of Lincoln.

> I should only be too glad if the Mayor thought it worth while to make use of any notes of mine on the occasion referred to—but alas, I have no time to write any just now, except only that I have always held (and am prepared against all comers to maintain my holding) that the Cathedral of Lincoln is out and out the most precious piece of architecture in the British islands, and—roughly—worth any two other cathedrals we have got;—secondly, that the town of Lincoln is a lovely old English town, and I hope the Mayor and Common Council men won't let any of it (not so much as a house corner) be pulled down

to build an Institution or a Market—or a Penitentiary or a Gunpowder and Dynamite Mill—or a College—or a Gaol—or a Barracks—or any other modern luxury. And thirdly, that it might possibly make the upper students of the art classes look up a good many things that they would be the better for knowing, if the Town Council were to offer a prize for a design to be painted or frescoed in the Town Hall, of the most pathetic and significant scene in all British history—the first real "Union of Scotland and England"—in the funeral procession of Bishop Hugh—when the King of England (John), barefoot, bore the coffin, with three Archbishops, and the King of Scotland followed, weeping. (See Froude's sketch of Bishop Hugo in the *Studies of Great Subjects*.2) The prize might be open to all students born between Lincoln and Holy Isle? — or better, perhaps, between Tweed and Trent?

With all good wishes for the prosperity and honour of your son's Mayoralty, and for its serviceable use to the good town of Lincoln, I am, my dear Sir, your faithful servant,

JOHN RUSKIN

In another piece, his critique on modern commercial practice was sharper:

Right and wrong uses of labour: If you are a young lady and employ a certain number of sempstresses for a given time in making a given number of simple and serviceable dresses, suppose seven, of which you can wear one yourself for half the winter, and give six away to poor girls who have none, you are spending your money unselfishly. But, if you employ the same

number of sempstresses for the same number of
days, in making four, or five, or six beautiful
flounces for your own ball dress - flounces which
will clothe no one but yourself, and which you
will yourself be unable to wear at more than one
ball - you are employing your money selfishly.
(Political Economy of Art, Lecture 1 page 2.) [300]

Ruskin consented to the production of the *Selections*, but, as the preface makes clear, he did not 'take any part in making the selections nor in the appearance of the volume'. In the Ruskin archive there is a letter from Thomas Carlyle to James Ruskin saying how wonderful he found it was to have the book at hand and available to dip into. He adds that for very many people who may not otherwise have access to Ruskin's works it was of huge value. Ruskin seems to have taken a rather different view.

The Complete Works of John Ruskin is an astonishing collection amounting to some thirty-eight volumes. In the Bibliographical Appendix there are some details about the *Selections*. Firstly, it is entirely clear that the selections were made by William Smith Williams. It was published on 18 November 1861 and there were several later reprints including a number of unauthorised editions, such as that by Routledge in the USA. John Ruskin's views of the *Selections* become apparent from his letters to his father: 'Don't send the book of extracts to anybody, that you can help. Above all – don't send it here. It is a form of mince-pie which I have no fancy for. My crest is all very well as long as it means pork, but I don't love being made into sausages.[301]' His father continues the food metaphor writing to his friend John Simon, 'You saw what Mr Harrison calls *our* volume, and I don't wonder that you do not like it. The sweets are brought together in cloying abundance, and the descriptions thickened into monotony'.[302]

Clement Shorter points out that, perhaps, this was not the whole story, and certainly not the view of Ruskin's mother:

TO W. S. WILLIAMS

Denmark Hill, 20th November, 1861.

My dear Sir, — I am requested by Mrs. Ruskin to return her very sincere and grateful thanks for your kind consideration in presenting her with so beautifully bound a copy of the Selections from her son's writings; and which she will have great pleasure in seeing by the side of the very magnificent volumes which the liberality of the gentlemen of your house has already enriched our library with.

Mrs. Ruskin joins me in offering congratulations on the great judgment you have displayed in your Selections, and, sending my own thanks and those of my son for the handsome gift to Mrs. Ruskin, — I am, my dear sir, yours very truly,

John James Ruskin.[303]

John Ruskin's relationship with Smith, Elder & Co. extended over a number of decades, and it would take more than a disagreement over one book to displace it. In 1862 Smith, Elder & Co. published *Unto this Last,* Ruskin's principal work on Political Economy, and which included the offending articles from The *Cornhill*. Andrew Ballantyne writes:

> Ruskin argued that conventional economics treated people as if they were covetous machines. If they were treated differently, they would behave differently. The motive force that drives things along is human will; there are souls in this machine, and it is most productive not when it is administered oppressively, but when people are in love with the thing they are doing and when they have proper respect for and from those

around them.[304]

Correspondence between William and Ruskin shows both that more books followed, but also that a cordial but robust relationship continued. These letters fall broadly between the death of Ruskin's father in 1864 and his appointment as Slade Professor at Oxford in 1870 which also coincided with a decline in his mental health.[305]

On 15 January 1864 he wrote:

Dear Mr Williams,

> I am ashamed at not having thanked you before for the Doyle book. I wanted to look at it carefully. It is full of power, but entirely wrong in feeling. A form of satire which will do no good, but there is wonderful work in it, and I am glad to have it. I liked the Manners and Customs far better, however, that I have had a long while as a classical work. My kindest regards to Mr Smith. – Always affectionately yours, J. Ruskin[306]

The Smith, Elder & Co. archive has some correspondence with an illustrator called Richard Doyle. He was the uncle of Arthur Conan Doyle, who too would be published by Smith, Elder & Co. Two letters in 1865 point to a more workmanlike relationship, and, with this, a rather more personal connection in November 1865:

Dear Mr Williams,

> I think the lecture looks and reads very nice. Perhaps people will say the pages are like my mother's mince pies this year - more edges than meat. I'll send you on Monday some of the first lecture, that we may set the types free, and I will correct this at leisure. It is beautifully correct for a first proof. My writing must be improving!! – Truly and affectionately yours, J Ruskin[307]

The more personal connection appears again at the end

of this letter from 1867:

Dear Mr Williams,

I am very much obliged to the printer to his correction - the word should be "treble" not "double". It gives me great pleasure to have a little word from you again, and I take the occasion to ask a question respecting Messrs. Routledge.

They have been teasing me to write for the *Broadway*. I positively refuse at present to write anything *for* anything. But I find my books, so far as read, also wholly misread, and - I won't say misunderstood (for there is no understanding to miss), but mis-swallowed in America, that they do no end of mischief. So I offered Messrs. Routledge, if they could make their peace with Messrs. Smith and Elder, to extract for them the facts of my books about Art which I wished chiefly to be read, with a comment or two to prevent indigestion, and some necessary rearrangement.

So they accepted and asked me to write to Mr King about it. I really want to do this, and unless I have some stimulus and poking periodically, I never shall. When it was all *done*, I would add some important new bits, put it all in better form - and then, if you liked, you should publish its yourselves, being the *practical* art of *Modern Painters* separated from the Criticism, Theology, "Natural" Descriptions, and Politics. You might make your own terms with Messrs. Routledge for the permission to have the bare extracts periodically. I shall charge nothing for these, nor add anything of importance till all is done.

My mother begs her kindest regards, - ever most

truly yours, J Ruskin[308]

The personal connection is perhaps confirmed by something William's youngest daughter, Anna, said in an interview on her retirement and when she recalled some of her childhood. "When my father was living we saw such a number of interesting people. Ruskin, Carlyle, Thackeray, Leigh Hunt, and so many others."

The mention again of Thomas Carlyle brings into view a remarkable little book that was written about the Carlyle family's Chelsea Home at 5 Cheyne Row.[309] In this, Reginald Blunt lists the many celebrated visitors. John Ruskin is among them but, he says, only from about 1860. This would make sense given that, in 1860, Anna was in her early teens and so fully aware of who visitors were.

The Ruskin letters I have so far referred to were all included in the volumes of the Complete Works. The Smith, Elder & Co. archive at the National Library of Scotland contains a further group of letters addressed personally to William by John Ruskin all concerning lectures, broadly, on Political Economy.[310] In these lectures, I believe, Ruskin was thinking aloud and it is important to remember one or two factors affecting his ideas. He was a committed Christian; he believed that great art was the expression of God's gifts. He was also desperately concerned about people. Whilst he spent a great deal of his time immersed in art and architecture, he did not fail to see what was going on around him. He witnessed industrialisation and, in particular, the way in which skills were being replaced by repetitive processes. This, he believed, dehumanised people and was too high a price to pay for progress. His thinking in relation to women is more complex. His mother was probably overly concerned for her son. His wife, Effe, failed in his eyes to match his ideal; Effe, for her part, suffered from his overbearing parents. Ruskin was much criticised for the failure of the marriage, nevertheless, he saw it his duty to champion the education of women. I believe that this thinking must have resonated strongly with William. It is important also to recognise the context in which Ruskin was writing. Living conditions for the great mass of the working population were quite dreadful. Working conditions for men were awful. The role of women, which had always been subservient, was being questioned, almost for the first time. The education of women was beginning to be taken seriously. Yet, despite the efforts of publishers to produce affordable books and that of the voluntary bodies in running schools, books were still unavailable to all but the privileged few.

The first of these letters is dated 24 March 1865 and it surprised me, for, if nothing else, when you read it, Ruskin is being serious. In the letter he is asking William's views on a title - *King's Treasuries and Queen's Gardens* - explaining that it was inspired bylines from the nursery rhyme: 'The King was in his counting house and the Queen was in the parlour'! All soon becomes clear. The first title was, in fact, two, one for each of two related essays which Ruskin had delivered in late 1864, the first on the role of men and the second on that of women. The book as a whole was not necessarily aimed at children, but it was certainly accessible by them. The whole book, eventually called *Sesame and Lilies,* proved extremely popular, selling 160,000 copies through numerous editions. It was frequently a Sunday School prize.[311] The editors of *The Complete Works of John Ruskin* add, in their introduction, some helpful background. They echo first the tension between Ruskin's vocation in art and his political concern for his fellow man and woman. The first of the lectures, The King's Treasures, was delivered in order to raise money for a public library in Manchester. The name 'Sesame' was derived from the well-known phrase 'open sesame'; Ruskin wanted to open the treasure of books - surely a wish which resonated strongly with William.

William had filled the role which he did so often with his authors, the father confessor, almost. The letter of 17

August 1865 suggests that, for Ruskin, writing was not all plain sailing. He writes 'The wild flowers are so beautiful that I can't write in the mornings and I'm always half-dead at night – so I can't get this preface done – besides, its difficult.'

Of course, the preface was done and the book published. It is now viewed as very dated particularly in its attitudes to women. However, a review in the *Journal of Education* in the USA as late as 1906 was thoroughly warm about it:

> "Sesame and Lilies" is one of the most attractive, wholesome, and important of British classics [...] these lectures present concisely some of the fundamental principles which characterised Ruskin's teaching. Not only is the work interesting in its contribution to the economic discussions of the time, but it is written in a style of great strength.[312]

It was republished by Yale in 2002. On 18 October 1865 following its original publication, Ruskin wrote to William about the next volume. Once again it was on the question of the title that he consulted William:

> I had not fixed on any name – and at first I tried to find a pretty one; but on the whole - as the subject is a dull one – (though I think I can make it a little amusing) it is best to promise nothing – people will find out if it is, in time – I think therefore of calling it
>
> The Ethics of Dust, Ten lectures to little Housewives
>
> The real subject (don't laugh) is crystallography. But if you can come out next Sunday at 1.00 part for to meet Mr Harrison, I'll read you a little bit of it, and you shall consult upon it.

The book, which indeed was called *The Ethics of the Dust*, came from lectures which Ruskin had delivered to Wilmington Hall girls' school near Nantwich in Cheshire. Its purpose was to teach crystallography, but also to explore the method of teaching girls. Once again the road to publication was not entirely straightforward. There was an issue over price.

3 November 1865

Dear Mr Williams,

I'm so glad to see you on your throne again. You know there's really no need of explanation about Sesame – I named a foolish price – and you and the firm allowed it – I never meant to lose money by the book – nor thought you would fix a price which would. Now it can't be helped; we must put a wise price if there is a new edition.

But the main thing is now.

I have brought you a chapter of my new book. Can you get it put into type for me, that I may see how it looks, that we may go on knowingly after we once begin.

I think the dialogue form will necessitate a somewhat wider and closer page than Sesame.

There are ten chapters most of them rather longer than this.'

William would, I think, have been fascinated by Ruskin's ideas. The book must also have brought back memories of his correspondence with Charlotte Brontë on the subject of girls' education. It is entirely possible that it was a subject of family discussion, too, since both Ruskin and Lowes Dickinson were teaching at the Working Men's College. W.G. Collingwood, in his *Life of John Ruskin*, expands a little on the teaching:

Ruskin's method of teaching, as illustrated in "Ethics of Dust", has been variously pooh-poohed by his critics. It has seemed to some absurd to mix Theology, and Crystallography, and Political Economy, and Mythology, and Moral Philosophy, with the chatter of school-girls and the romps of the playgrounds. But it should be understood, before reading this book, which is practically the report of these Wilmington talks, that it is printed as an illustration of a method. It showed that play-lessons need not want either depth or accuracy; and that the requirement was simply capacity on the part of the teacher.[313]

Thomas Carlyle in his letter to Ruskin of 20 December 1865 is full of praise for the work:

The Ethics of the Dust, which I devoured without pause, and intend to look at again, is a most shining Performance! Not for a long while have I read anything tenth-part so radiant with talent, ingenuity, lambent fire (sheet and other lightnings) of all commendable kinds! Never was such a Lecture on Crystallography before had there been nothing else in it, and there are all manner of things. In power of expression, I pronounce it to be supreme; never did anybody who had such things to explain, explain them better. And the bits of Egyptian Mythology, the cunning Dreams about Pthah, Neith, etc., apart from their elucidative quality, which is exquisite, have in them a poetry that might fill any Tennyson with despair. You are very dramatic, too; nothing wanting in the stage-directions, in the pretty little indications—a very pretty stage and dramatis personæ altogether. Such is my first feeling about your book, dear R. Come soon, and I will tell you all the faults of it, if I gradually discover a great many. In fact, come at any rate!

Yours ever,

T. CARLYLE.[314]

March 1866 saw the beginning of the path to publication, initially, of two further lectures. One was given to a working men's college near Denmark Hill, where Ruskin lived, and concerned the issues about the contemporary workplace that troubled Ruskin so. He hated the way repetitive work dehumanised craftsmen. The other was delivered to the Royal Military Academy at Woolwich and was on the highly topical subject of war. The Crimean War had ended some ten years before, but war was very much in the air on the continent, in Italy which held an important place in the minds of the British liberals. The lecture, though, seems to have been well received, since Ruskin asked for fifty copies of the lecture to be printed separately for distribution at Woolwich. These two lectures along with a third were published together under the title *The Crown of the Wild Olive*.

Ruskin wrote on 5 March 1866:

> The two lectures will be sent to Mr King by Wednesday morning and should be printed as for Sesame and the Lilies but price at 5 shillings. I am going to say something in the preface about the article in the Pall Mall yesterday: Education 1,000,000 Fighting 25,000,000

The numbers quoted are almost certainly those for propose government expenditure.

A letter of 3 November implies that William might have been absent and this of the following 16 August confirms that absences must have taken place. The reason may have been that William's youngest son Thornton Arthur, a merchant's clerk, married Elizabeth Baumer at Hampstead Parish Church on 21 June 1866.

The August letter also brings out again a more personal

side to the relationship and possibly differing views on the relative popularity of the books.

16 August 1866

I am glad to see your hand again and should like to see your face, but my mother is not very well just now - are you remaining in touch with her? I should like you to come over on Sunday fortnight when I hope she will be quite well.

I should like to see you publish any of my books on political economy in any way you like best. I never expected them to sell; but wrote them for foundations of future work. But I <u>did</u> expect Ethics of the Dust to sell, and am a little disappointed that you think it so much a matter of congratulations to me that you are still asked for it. I am sure that no introduction to mineralogy for children is better of its kind and I fancied it was amusing besides, but I suppose it isn't.

This letter was to be followed by a gap in the archive of three years where William might have been absent and letters were exchanged impersonally with the firm.

William and Margaret had moved to 6 Chepstow Villas, Avenue Road, Twickenham where, after a long wait, William would at last be qualified to vote, as a result of the 1867 Reform Act. William, I am sure, would have keenly followed it parliamentary progress and would have been aware of the petition demanding votes for women presented to Parliament in July 1866. He would have exercise his right to vote in the General Election of November 1868 which returned Gladstone with an increased Liberal majority.

It is likely that worries at home had also preoccupied him. Ellen, William's little granddaughter who had been listed on their 1861 census return and had been part of their household, died in 1868 of liver disease.

William had later returned to active work for on 20 September 1869, Ruskin writes:

> Many thanks for your letters. I am very glad to have a personality to write to...I have been thinking over this matter and I believe we might at once go forward sure of Mr Smith's approval thus...I wish now to publish a series of my work, old and new –

This first task though was the next book, *Time and Tide*, which Ruskin mentions in his letter of 23 September, adding that he hoped it would cover costs. Collingwood explains that *Time and Tide* was a 'series of letters addressed to Thomas Dixon a working cork-cutter of Sunderland.[315]' I wonder whether there is a Brontë echo here? William was described by Charlotte to her friend Mary Taylor in a letter of 4 September 1848 as 'a pale stooping man of fifty very much like a faded Tom Dixon'.

Ruskin's next letter is from the Shortest Day of 1870, and he writes to William of the need to make the most of days, short and long. There is a new edition of *Sesame,* and Ruskin is working on the preface to a new book of two hundred pages. Then, on 28 December, Ruskin writes of his pleasure at the new pamphlet, asking William to send it to the 'usual journals' and a further one thousand copies to Mr Allen. George Allen was a man whom Ruskin taught at the Working Men's College and who had engraved for him. Now Allen was to undertake the distribution of Ruskin's new venture, *Fors Clavigera*, which was a monthly publication in the form of letters to the working men and labourers of England.[316] Collingwood adds that readers of *Fors* will need no further introduction to their old acquaintance the tallow-chandler. I just wonder if Ruskin had taken this from conversations with William about his father's occupation? Ruskin's friend Thomas Carlyle wrote this about *Fors* in a letter of 30 April 1871:

Dear Ruskin,

This *Fors Clavigera*, which I have just finished reading, is incomparable; a quasi-sacred consolation to me, which almost brings tears into my eyes! Every word of it is as if spoken, not out of my poor heart only, but out of the eternal skies; words winged with Empyrean wisdom, piercing as lightning, - and which I really do not remember to have heard the like of.

Ruskin's letters to William of January and April 1871 concern the compilation of the series of his work including *Illumera Pulviris*. Ruskin adds that he wants William to publish it rather than Macmillan. This was the last of Ruskin's works published by Smith, Elder & Co., from then on he took on the publishing of his own work with George Allen.

The 1871 census return (the last of William's life) from Chepstow Villas recorded William and Margaret with Richard and Anna (once again living at home), his daughter Mary (Tiny) and two of William's grandchildren Louis Robertson and Frank Williams then aged thirteen. Frank's father (William's son) it seems had disappeared from the scene, for, in 1862, Ellen had married Frank Deacon, a relation of the Deacons already mentioned.

A further marriage took place in 1871, when Emily Williams's other sister, Laura, married celebrated artist and Royal Academician Sir Lawrence Alma-Tadema. Young Frank Williams was listed as present at this wedding and, as I tell in the next chapter, it obviously made quite an impression. William and Margaret's third son, Richard, and youngest daughter, Anna, would both marry after William's death.

Anna had from 1870 been studying with HC Deacon, William's friend. She told her interviewer, F Klickmann, on her retirement, that hers was the smallest voice of all her siblings and so when she announced that she was going to study in Italy there was consternation. Nonetheless she went and, following a period of study, she began her performing career. There is a letter dated 10 February 1873 from Charles Hill's wife writing to her sister-in-law, Sophia, in which she reports:

> Our dear sister Margaret kindly came to us see not long since, bringing Tiny's son with her. She looks well and was so kind. Anna sang at the Crystal Palace a fortnight since. I went to hear her and was much pleased and I enjoyed meeting this many of the family. Ellen, Tiny, Dick and Arthur, Mr Williams ...not there having a cold but he is better.

William kept working into his seventies. In the archive, there is one letter from this period and it is from Millicent Fawcett, the women's suffrage campaigner and sister of one of those involved in the Langham Place Group, and is dated 27 December 1874. Mrs Fawcett had sent to William a story entitled, *Janet Doncaster*, and she was concerned that readers might think of her rather better known works on Political Economy and the role of women and so might be confused if a story were published in her name. It was published as novel under her name in 1875 and has only recently been re-issued.

William retired from Smith, Elder & Co. in early 1875, with his place being taken by James Payn, a novelist, whose taste 'lay in a lighter form of literature'.[317]

12 LEGACY

William and Margaret's retirement to Twickenham was both short-lived and also not really retirement. In the final months of William's life, he wrote letters trying to once more secure the republication of *Joseph and His Brethren*, written by his life long friend Charles Wells. In response, Algernon Charles Swinburne wrote to William on 15 March 1875:

My dear sir

I ought to have thanked you before now for the letter which you forwarded to me from Mr Wells, to whom I must also write a word of acknowledgement, and also for the very kind expressions of your note accompanying it. I am sincerely glad if I have been able to do any additional service to the fame of the noble poem which I have admired too many years, and which I am happy to hear is at last about to have a fresh start with the public. I consider it a great honour to be in any way associated with its revival and, as it were, to act as outrider or usher to what I hope will prove the triumphal car of a poet too long defrauded of his just crown of praise.

I remain my dear Sir

Yours very sincerely, AC Swinburne[318]

Joseph and His Brethren was published the following year by Chatto and Windus with an introduction by Algernon Swinburne.

William Smith Williams died at his home in Twickenham on 26 August 1875, of prostatic hypertrophy and senile dementia.[319] He was buried in Kensal Green Cemetery in the same grave as his son Robert. The remains of his daughter Ellen and his wife would join his in 1882 and 1888. The adjacent grave would contain the remains of his son-in-law, Lowes Dickinson, and his daughter Fanny Emily. The grave is marked by a monument designed by A.C. Gill.

With thanks to Brian Speak

His brother-in-law, Robert Hill, wrote to his sister

Sophia with the news not only of William's death but also that of two other in-laws. Of Mr Williams, he wrote first: 'Poor Mr Williams had been failing some time but we were not apprehensive of anything fatal till a few days before his death when he gradually sank and died on the 26 August surrounded by all his family. I don't know what his illness was said to be but suppose it was simply the decay of nature as he was 75 years of age!' He then added, 'Poor Mr Williams was buried in the cemetery at Kensal Green near the graves of Robert and Mr Robertson, Tiny's husband, all his children followed, in addition Sidney Moxsy, Francis Hill, Lowes Dickinson, his eldest son, Tiny's son and myself, besides some friends. There were complimentary notices of his death in nearly all the papers. Nobody could have been more universally beloved or respected than he was, so we pass away one after another!'[320]

A number of obituaries appeared after William's death. *The Athenaeum*, for which he had written over many years, described his career and said:

> In reading this announcement many will feel they have lost the most agreeable and valued friend and a real feeling of sorrow will be felt by a wide literary circle; for in the course of his duties Mr Williams was necessarily brought into the immediate relations with very many of the literary celebrities of his time, and his well-known gentleman-like and engaging manner and obliging disposition endeared him to all who had dealings with him. His literary taste was excellent, and he had great powers of discernment. His judgement and his opinion regarding the works was very highly valued, more especially by young authors.

The Publishers Circular added this, writing of his work at Smith, Elder & Co.:

> Here his work was found for him, humble and

unpretentious it is true, but of immense importance to authors and publishers. The task of reading and selecting, and we may presume that, genial as Mr Williams was - he rejected at least scores of volumes to one he accepted - became so absorbed that he ceased to write himself, and hence became more warmly friendly with many writers whose names are known to all the world and whose friendship and esteem he never lost. Amongst these may be named Leigh and Thornton Hunt, WM Thackeray, the Miss Brontës, John Ruskin, Miss Kavanagh, Mrs Parr (Holme Lee), Egerton Webbe, George Henry Lewes and many others including a great number of painters.

After William's death, Margaret moved to 1 St Leonards Villas, Hanwell, near to her daughter and son-in-law Lowes Dickinson. Mary and Louis Robertson were recorded in the 1881 census as still living there with her.

Margaret Williams - with thanks to Cheryl Pivac

In 1879, Lowes Dickinson and Ellen moved into a newly-built house at No. 1, All Souls Place, Langham

Place, Hanwell. In his biography of Goldsworthy Lowes Dickinson, E.M. Forster sheds some helpful light on Lowes Dickinson and his family.[321] After a demanding day in his studio, he tells how Lowes Dickinson would come home and read 'Scott, Shakespeare or Coleridge aloud to his children'. Forster tells how the marriage of Lowes Dickinson and Ellen Williams was 'supremely happy', which, he suggests, brought Goldie to regard marriage as 'the best attainable earthly state'. Ellen was a woman of 'sweet but firm character, with strong opinions as to what was right and wrong, and with a narrow vein of piety running through the abundance of her natural goodness'. In his autobiography, Goldie remembers his mother's 'long chestnut hair reaching almost to her feet when it was let down.[322]'

Lowes Dickinson had sent his sons to Charterhouse, from where they both went to King's College, Cambridge. Arthur gained a first in Maths. He went on to become an accountant, soon becoming a partner in the London firm of Lovelock, Whiffin & Dickinson. Through an involvement with a Californian company, he came to know Nicholas Waterhouse, son of one of the founders of Price Waterhouse. At that time, the American firm associated with Price Waterhouse was thriving, but it had lost both of its lead partners. Waterhouse asked Dickinson to go to New York to take charge. Arthur sailed on 1 April 1900 and took up his post on I July. He would serve the American firm until 1909 when he declared his wish to return to London. The death of his father in that year might have had some influence on this. In his eight years, the firm achieved prodigious growth, opening offices in San Francisco, Mexico City, Seattle, Montreal, Boston and Toronto. He also played a major role in the US accounting profession. All this came at a cost of a breakdown in his health. Sir Nicholas Waterhouse described him as 'a man of terrific and unbounded energy' and as having 'the kindest and most sympathetic disposition'.[323] Like a number of partners in Price Waterhouse, in 1915, Arthur volunteered to the war effort and served the Ministry of Munitions as financial adviser to the controlled establishment division. This division managed the factories around the country which had devoted production to the war effort.[324] Arthur, together with five other Price Waterhouse partners, was awarded a knighthood for his war work.

Goldie Lowes Dickinson became a fellow of King's College, Cambridge. He wrote very extensively. Many of his books were published by George Allen, but none by Smith, Elder & Co. Among his books are editions of Carlyle's *French Revolution* and his *Sartor Resarus*. Neither his biography nor autobiography say more than is generally known about his maternal grandfather. He, though, is best known as one of the leading thinkers behind the League of Nations. His friend and biographer E.M. Forster wrote of his feeling when the Great War broke out, saying that they were best conveyed by analogy:

> They resemble feelings which arise when a promise has been broken by a person whom one loves. One knows all the time that the promise will not be kept, perhaps cannot be kept, yet the shock is none the less mortal.[325]

Goldie himself explained that he was not a conscientious objector. He had considered joining the Friends Ambulance Corps, but had concluded that what he did should be of a different kind: 'I devoted myself, so far as there was any opportunity for such work, to propaganda for a League of Nations'. I can't help hearing echoes of William.

Frank Williams (junior) returned to Australia where he married Julia Montgomery on 18 July 1883 and had three daughters Amelia Vera (Vera) born in 1885 in Walgett, Dorothy born in 1887 in Walgett, and Erica Thornton born in Taree in 1891. Amelia was nicknamed 'Tad' by her father, after Sir Lawrence Alma-Tadema; that wedding that Frank had attended clearly had made an impression. There are descendants still living in Australia, not least those kind enough to provide me with much family information. Frank was also an accountant, with the Bank of New South Wales.

Mary Louisa (Tiny) spent most of her life as a widow. She was a letter writer and a number of her letters to her aunt Sophia in Australia have been made available to me by Sophia's descendent Cheryl Pivac. Her letter of 27 April 1890 offers a wonderful memory of William doing what he loved most: 'I went to the Royal Academy saw the Pictures. Lowes has three. They're in the New gallery which is smaller and[…] more in consequence. But, nature beats all pictures. I am like Father walking about feeling, if not saying, "lovely, lovely" and I always feel his spirit near me.'[326]

Fanny Emily continued to teach music after she was left by her husband. In the 1881 census, she was recorded as living as a boarder at 17 Eastgate, Lincoln. In 1891, shortly before she died, she was back in London living with her sister, Anna. Reading the letters to her aunt Sophia, it seems that she remained an unhappy person. Emily Epps Williams, like her sister-in-law, was also a widow for most of her life. She was an artist, but she produced hardy any work after her husband's death. Richard Smith Williams became an accountant and married Marian McKenzie, who had been one of Anna's pupils and who also pursued a career as a vocalist and teacher. I have a note in our family archive that Marian taught music to my father's first wife.

Arthur Thornton became a partner with Alston Hamilton & Co, London and Ceylon Merchants. My father recalled that, in 1912, he went to an interview with Thornton for a job as an assistant on a rubber estate in Malaya. My father did indeed go out to Malaya, and worked on the Elphil Rubber Estate. Thornton and

Elizabeth had two children, a daughter, Annette Baumer Williams, born around 1868 (who married a solicitor Macrae Moir) and a son, Philip Hamilton Williams, born in March 1874. Philip also was a chartered accountant and became renowned as an English chess problemist and chess author.[327] Annette had two children: a son, Kenneth Macrae Moir, in 1895 who became a solicitor at the same London firm as his father, and a daughter, Betty, in 1900.[328] As we have seen, it was Thornton who had custody of Charlotte Brontë's letters and it was Elizabeth who wrote about them for *The Macmillan Magazine*. Christine Hutchison adds that it was Thornton who had provided the information for the death certificate of his little niece Ellen.

William's youngest daughter, Anna, went on to become a celebrated oratorio soprano.

Anna Williams from Moments with Modern Musicians

She sang with Richter and with Charles Hallé. Klickmann met her in her house in northwest London and noted that, unlike many prima donnas, there were none of the usual photographs of her with famous musicians. He noticed some fine paintings including a number by Lowes Dickinson. Anna went on to teach singing at the Royal

College of Music. She married Rodney Fennessey on 23 July 1910 just five years before his death. She died on 3 September 1924 in London. Her death was reported widely, including in Australian newspapers. Her obituary, by her colleague and friend, Florence A Cecil-Smith, told how 'she carried the same enthusiasm and energy into anything she undertook in her private life, inspiring everyone who came in contact with her by her fine intellectual qualities and tastes, her alert brain and wide-mindedness, her unselfishness and thought for others, her great generosity in its never failing response to the troubles and needs of those who were sometimes hardly acquaintances, and finally her splendid pluck and courage. In looking back I can find nothing in her character I did not revere, and consider one of the privileges of my life that we were such great friends'.[329] Surely there are echoes of her father?

In the Brontë archive at Haworth there is a very large family tree having at its head Francis Hill of Broxbourne.[330] It lists at the top those thought to have been significant:

Marian McKenzie – celebrated contralto singer

Kenneth Macrae Moir – War Service 1914-1919 – Capt. East Surrey Regt. Subsequently Machine Gun Corps

Arthur Rupert Moxsy – War Service 1914-1919 – Major Inniskilling Fusiliers – Military Cross

Charles Wells (senior) – poet "Stories after Nature" "Joseph and His Brethren" Friend of Keats

William Smith Williams – Literary critic

Thornton Arthur Williams – partner in Alston Hamilton & Co, London and Ceylon Merchants

Anna Williams – celebrated soprano singer

The author of the tree could have added, for War Service 1914-1919, my father Leslie Hamlyn Williams, William's great nephew, who was Commissioned in the Suffolk Regiment and went on to serve in the Army Ordnance Department and was awarded a Military Cross for devotion to duty.

He could also have mentioned Charles Wells's son, Charles Deville Wells who became an inventor and was notorious later as the 'man who broke the bank at Monte Carlo'. I ought to add that my own grandfather, Alfred Hamlyn Williams, was also an inventor and was said to have lost money at Monte Carlo. I wonder whether he and Charles ever met? I am indebted to Robin Quinn for his research into, and book on, *The Man Who Broke the Bank at Monte Carlo*. In this he traces the life and work of Charles Deville Wells. I am relieved to say that his book makes no mention of my grandfather, who was both a far less prodigious inventor and far more modest gambler. Wells was prodigious in both. Quinn tells how, between 1885 and 1892, he made some one hundred and ninety-two patent applications. He then tells the story of how Wells came to break the bank. He is less kind about Charles Jeremiah Wells than I have been and highlights a rather large amount of money (£1,000) that Wells borrowed from Richard Hengist Horne which was never repaid. Quinn also quotes Horne as saying of Wells: 'he has no industry or perseverance. He was the idlest man I ever knew, and the most gifted'. He quotes William as saying, 'He was a most dangerous and insidious person'.[331] To me, the contrast between this and William's tireless efforts with *Joseph and His Brethren* rather underlines William's kind and forgiving nature.

William's most enduring legacy was, surely, *Jane Eyre*, and this continues to be read and loved by succeeding generations. I wonder, though, whether his wise encouragement to so many writers and artists has also been absorbed into our artistic heritage.

ABOUT THE AUTHOR

Philip Hamlyn Williams came to write biography following careers in the accounting profession (Partner in Price Waterhouse) and the not for profit sector, most recently as Chief Executive of Lincoln Cathedral (2011-2014). In 2008/2009, he took an MA in Professional Writing at University College Falmouth, having then recently completed a distance learning BA at The University Exeter for which he was awarded a First Class Honours Degree. His first books drew on a family archive of material and extensive additional research: *Ordnance – Equipping the Army for the Great War*, was published by The History Press in June 2018 and followed a companion book on WW2, *War on Wheels*, which had, as its focus, the people who mechanised the army. In between writing these books, he was commissioned, by The Story Terrace, to write the *MacRobert's Reply* in collaboration with the son of the sole survivor of the crash, in 1941, of the Stirling Aircraft bearing the MacRobert name.

He is chair of the Lincoln Arts Trust which has the care and running of Lincoln Drill Hall (Lincoln's community arts centre). He also chairs the Lincoln Book Festival.

[1] David Cannadine, *Victorious Century*, (London: Allen Lane, 2017), p.10.
[2] David Cannadine, *Victorious Century*, (London: Allen Lane, 2017), p.132.
[3] Eric Hobsbawm, *Age of Revolution*, (London: Weidenfeld & Nicolson, 1962, Kindle Edition), loc. 1535
[4] David Cannadine, *Victorious Century*, (London: Allen Lane, 2017), p.14.
[5] Jerry White, *London in the 19th Century*, (London: Vintage, 2008), p.26.
[6] David Cannadine, *Victorious Century*, (London: Allen Lane, 2017), p.88.
[7] Eric Hobsbawm, *The Age of Revolution*, (London: Weidenfeld & Nicolson, 1962, Kindle Edition), loc. 645
[8] David Cannadine, *Victorious Century*, (London: Allen Lane, 2017), p.97.
[9] *Thomas Carlyle Selected Writings*, ed. by Alan Shelston, (London: Penguin Classics, 2015, Kindle Edition), loc. 120
[10] Theodore Watts-Dunton, *Rossetti and Charles Wells: A Reminiscence of Kelmscott Manor,* (1908), p.xlii.
[11] John Prest, *The Most Difficult Village*, (Oxford: Nuffield Press, 2006), p.12.
[12] Adrian Desmond and James Moore, *Darwin*, (London: Michael Joseph, 1991), p.492.
[13] John Prest, *The Most Difficult Village*, (Oxford: Nuffield Press, 2006) p.7.
[14] *The Letters of Charlotte Brontë, Volume 2: 1848-1851*, ed. by Margaret Smith, (Oxford: Clarendon Press, 2000), p.668.
[15] John Prest, *The Most Difficult Village*, (Oxford: Nuffield Press, 2006) p.7.
[16] Information kindly provided by the Wheatley Village Archive
[17] Information kindly provided by the Wheatley Village Archive

[18] Norman E. Penty, *The Discovery of Charlotte Brontë: William Smith Williams, 1800–1875: a Genealogical Quest,* (Private Circulation, 2006) I am grateful to Penty for his fascinating research into Smith Williams's family background and career.

[19] Jerry White, *London in the 19th Century*, (London: Vintage, 2008), p.101.

[20] Jerry White, *London in the 19th Century*, (London: Vintage, 2008), p.101.

[21] Jerry White, *London in the 19th Century*, (London: Vintage, 2008), p.14.

[22] Norman E. Penty, *The Discovery of Charlotte Brontë: William Smith Williams, 1800–1875: a Genealogical Quest,* (Private Circulation, 2006) p.4.

[23] Norman E Penty, *The Discovery of Charlotte Brontë: William Smith Williams 1800-1875 A Genealogical Quest*, (Private circulation, 2006), p.3.

[24] Norman E Penty, *The Discovery of Charlotte Brontë: William Smith Williams 1800-1875 A Genealogical Quest*, (Private Circulation, 2006), p.3.

[25] David Cannadine, *Victorious Century*, (London: Allen Lane, 2017), p.72.

[26] David Cannadine, *Victorious Century*, (London: Allen Lane, 2017), p.86.

[27] Michael Williams, *Some London Theatres Past and Present*, (London: Sampson Low & Co., 1883), p.120.

[28] Jerry White, *London in the 19th Century*, (London: Vintage, 2008), p.267.

[29] Norman E Penty, *The Discovery of Charlotte Brontë, William Smith Williams 1800-1875 A Genealogical Quest*, (Private Circulation, 2006), p.2.

[30] *The Letters of Charlotte Brontë, Volume 2: 1848-1851*, ed. by Margaret Smith, (Oxford: Clarendon Press, 2000), p.667.

[31] Paul F Mattheisen, 'Gosse's Candid "Snapshots"', *Victorian Studies*, VIII, 1965, pp.329–354.

[32] Norman E Penty, *The Discovery of Charlotte Brontë: William*

[32] *Smith Williams 1800-1875 A Genealogical Quest*, (Private Circulation 2006), p.7.
[33] Theodore Watts-Dunton, *Rossetti and Charles Wells: A Reminiscence of Kelmscott Manor,* (1908), p.xliii.
[34] Aileen Fyfe, *Steam-Powered Knowledge*, (Chicago: Chicago, 2012), p.19.
[35] Aileen Fyfe, *Steam-Powered Knowledge*, (Chicago: Chicago, 2012), p.32.
[36] Aileen Fyfe, *Steam-Powered Knowledge*, (Chicago: Chicago, 2012), p.19.
[37] John Dickinson and Company, 1896, 8
[38] Aileen Fyfe, *Steam-Powered Knowledge*, (Chicago: Chicago, 2012), p.32.
[39] John Dickinson and Company, 1896, 8
[40] Aileen Fyfe, *Steam-Powered Knowledge*, (Chicago: Chicago, 2012), p.34.
[41] Aileen Fyfe, *Steam-Powered Knowledge*, (Chicago: Chicago, 2012), p.4.
[42] Edmund Blunden, *Keats's Publisher: A Memoir of John Taylor*, (London: Cape, 1936)
[43] Edmund Blunden, *Keats's Publisher: A Memoir of John Taylor*, (London: Cape, 1936), p.26.
[44] Edmund Blunden, *Keats's Publisher: A Memoir of John Taylor*, (London: Cape, 1936), p.29.
[45] http://www.philsoc.org.uk/history.asp, accessed 6 November 2018
[46] Nicholas Roe, *Fiery Heart: The First Life of Leigh Hunt*, (London: Pimlico 2005), p.287.
[47] Nicholas Roe, *Fiery Heart: The First Life of Leigh Hunt,,* (London: Pimlico 2005), p.176.
[48] June Steffenson Hagen, *Tennyson and his publishers,* (London: Macmillan, 1979), p27.
[49] Antonia Fraser, Cromwell – our Chief of Men, (London: Weidenfeld & Nicolson, 1973), p.8.
[50] Edmund Blunden, *Keats's Publisher: A memoir of John Taylor*, (London: Cape, 1936), p.50.

[51] Theodore Watts-Dunton, *Rossetti and Charles Wells: a Reminiscence of Kelmscott Manor,* (1908), p.xliv.

[52] Norman E Penty, *The Discovery of Charlotte Brontë, William Smith Williams 1800-1875 A Genealogical Quest,* (Private Circulation ,2006), p.6.

[53] The Guardian Long Read, 16 November 1917

[54] Jane Robinson, *Hearts and Minds – The Untold Story of the Great Pilgrimage and How Women Won the Vote,* (London: Doubleday2018), p.18.

[55] Michael F Suarez and Sarah M. Zimmerman. 'John Clare's Career, "Keats's Publisher" and the Early Nineteenth-Century English Book Trade.' *Studies in Romanticism,* vol. 45, no. 3, 2006, pp. 377–396.

[56] William Hone, *The Table Book* volume II, no 39 (1827).

[57] Norman E Penty, *The Discovery of Charlotte Brontë: William Smith Williams 1800-1875 A Genealogical Quest,* (Private Circulation, 2006), p.7.

[58] With thanks to Fran Manning in New South Wales

[59] Cheryl Pivac has kindly provided copies of these letters.

[60] Theodore Watts-Dunton, *Rossetti and Charles Wells: A Reminiscence of Kelmscott Manor,* (1908), p.xx

[61] https://www.thelondonmagazine.org/about-us/

[62] Thomas Carlyle, *Selected Writings,* ed. by Alan Shelston (London: Penguin Classics, 2015, Kindle Edition), loc.80.

[63] Norman E Penty, *The Discovery of Charlotte Brontë: William Smith Williams 1800-1875 A Genealogical Quest,* (Private Circulation, 2006), p.7.

[64] David Cannadine, *Victorious Century,* (London: Allen Lane, 2017,) p.133.

[65] M. Brégeaut, *A Manual of Lithography, Clearly Explaining the Whole Art, and the Accidents that May Happen in Printing, with the Different Methods of Avoiding Them,* trans. by C Hullmandel, 3rd Edition, (Longman, Paternoster Row 1832)

[66] Jerry White, *London in the 19th Century,* (London: Vintage, 2008), p68.

67 Norman E Penty, *The Discovery of Charlotte Brontë, William Smith Williams 1800-1875 A Genealogical Quest*, (Private Circulation, 2006), p.9.
68 Hertfordshire Mercury, June 2, 1888.
69 Jerry White, *London in the 19th Century*, (London: Vintage, 2008) p.21.
70 Susanna Avery-Quash, "Making Britain Healthy, Wealthy and Wise: Henry Cole and the Society of Arts." *RSA Journal*, CXLVI (1998), pp. 126–129.
71 Elizabeth Bonythorn and Anthony Burton, *The Great Exhibitor: The Life and Work of Henry Cole,* (London: V&A, 2003), p.68.
72 William Smith Williams, *On Lithography*, (London: Society of Arts, 1847).
73 Andrew Ballantyne, *John Ruskin*, (London: Reaktion Books, 2015, Kindle Edition), loc. 438.
74 Leonard Huxley, *The House of Smith Elder*, (London: Private Circulation, 1923, Kindle Edition), loc. 858.
75 *The Works of John Ruskin*, ed. by E.T. Cook and Alexander Wedderburn, (London: George Allen, 1903), III, p.216.
76 William Smith Williams, *On Lithography*, (London: Society of Arts, 1847), p.233.
77 William Smith Williams, *On Lithography*, (London: Society of Arts, 1847), p.233.
78 William Smith Williams, *On Lithography*, (London: Society of Arts, 1847), p.234.
79 William Smith Williams, *On Lithography*, (London: Society of Arts, 1847), p.234.
80 William Smith Williams, *On Lithography*, (London: Society of Arts, 1847), p.235.
81 *The Letters of Charles Dickens*, Volume 2:1840-1841, ed.by Madeline House and Graham Storey,(Oxford: Clarendon Press,1969), p.134.
82 Dictionary of National Biography, 1885-1900, vol 52.
83 William Smith Williams, 'Fine Arts', *Athenaeum*, no. 792,

31 December 1842.
[84] William Smith Williams, 'Fine Arts', *Athenaeum*, no. 817, 24 June 1843, p597.
[85] William Smith Williams, 'Fine Arts', *Athenaeum*, no. 806, 8 April 1843. p.345.
[86] William Smith Williams, 'Fine Arts', *Athenaeum*, no. 798, 11 Feb 1843, p.141.
[87] William Smith Williams, 'Our Weekly Gossip', *Athenaeum*, no 834, 21 October, p.947.
[88] William Smith Williams, 'Music and Drama' *Athenaeum*, no. 835, 28 Oct 1843, p965.
[89] William Smith Williams, 'Fine Arts', *Athenaeum*, 23 Dec 1843 no. 843, p1139.
[90] Jerry White, *London in the 19th Century*, (London: Vintage, 2008), p.30.
[91] David Cannadine, *Victorious Century*, Allan Lane, 2017, p.242.
[92] The Letters of Charlotte Brontë: Volume 2: 1848-1851, ed. by Margaret Smith, (Oxford: Clarendon Press, 2000), p.116.
[93] Eileen Fauset, *The politics of writing, Julia Kavanagh*, (Manchester: Manchester University Press, 2009), p.17.
[94] Darwin Correspondence Project, "Letter no. 740,", http://www.darwinproject.ac.uk/DCP-LETT-740 accessed on 2 January 2018
[95] *The Letters of Charlotte Brontë, Volume 2: 1848-1851*, ed. by Margaret Smith, (Oxford: Clarendon Press, 2000), p.li.
[96] Leonard Huxley, *The House of Smith Elder*, (London: Private Circulation, 1923, Kindle Edition), Loc. 86.
[97] Leonard Huxley, *The House of Smith Elder*, (London: Private Circulation, 1923, Kindle Edition), loc. 256.
[98] Leonard Huxley, *The House of Smith Elder*, (London: Private Circulation, 1923, Kindle Edition), loc. 173, as confirmed in correspondence with the Merchant Taylor's Company.
[99] Leonard Huxley, *The House of Smith Elder*, (London:

Private Circulation, 1923, Kindle Edition) loc. 394.

[100] Elizabeth Smith, *George Smith: A Memoir with Some Pages of Autobiography*, (Private Circulation, 1902, Kindle Edition), loc. 113.

[101] Leonard Huxley, *The House of Smith Elder*, (London: Private Circulation, 1923, Kindle Edition), loc. 589.

[102] Theodore Watts-Dunton, *Rossetti and Charles Wells: a reminiscence of Kelmscott Manor*, (1908), p.lv.

[103] Leonard Huxley, *The House of Smith Elder*, (London: Private Circulation, 1923, Kindle Edition), loc. 609.

[104] Leonard Huxley, *The House of Smith Elder*, (London: Private Circulation, 1923, Kindle Edition), loc. 643.

[105] Leonard Huxley, *The House of Smith Elder*, (London: Private Circulation, 1923, Kindle Edition), loc. 655.

[106] Elizabeth Smith, *George Smith: A Memoir with Some Pages of Autobiography*, (Private Circulation, 1902, Kindle Edition), loc. 226.

[107] Elizabeth Smith, *George Smith: A Memoir with Some Pages of Autobiography*, (Private Circulation, 1902, Kindle Edition),

[108] Andrew Ballantyne, *John Ruskin*, (London: Reaktion Books, 2015, Kindle Edition), loc. 470.

[109] Timothy Hilton, *The Pre-Raphaelites*, (London: Thames and Hudson, 1970), p.15.

[110] *The Letters of Charlotte Brontë, Volume 2: 1848-1851*, ed. by Margaret Smith, (Oxford: Clarendon Press, 2000), p.85.

[111] Elizabeth Smith, *George Smith: A Memoir with Some Pages of Autobiography*, (Private Circulation, 1902, Kindle Edition), loc. 1256

[112] Franklin Gary, Charlotte Brontë and George Henry Lewes." *PMLA*, LI (1936), pp. 518–542.

[113] *The Letters of Charlotte Brontë, Volume 2: 1848-1851*, ed. by Margaret Smith, (Oxford: Clarendon Press, 2000), p.112.

[114] Susan Magarey, *Unbridling the Tongues of Women: A Biography of Catherine Helen Spence*, (South Australia: University of Adelaide Press, 2010), pp. 43–62.

[115] Gordon S. Haight, *George Eliot: A Biography*, (Oxford: Clarendon Press, 1968), p.132.
[116] The Times, 8 September 1924 page 17.
[117] William Michael Rossetti, *Some Reminiscences*, (New York: Schribner, 1906), p.97.
[118] Norman E Penty, *The Discovery of Charlotte Brontë, William Smith Williams 1800-1875 A Genealogical Quest*, (Private Circulation, 2006), p.9.
[119] Eileen Fauset, *The Politics of Writing: Julia Kavanagh*, (Manchester: Manchester University Press, 2009), p.15.
[120] Eileen Fauset, *The Politics of Writin:, Julia Kavanagh*, (Manchester: Manchester University Press, 2009,) p.5.
[121] Charlotte Brontë to William Smith Williams, 7 August 1847, Brontë Society SG3.
[122] Rebecca Fraser, *Charlotte Brontë*, (London: Methuen, 1988), p.276.
[123] Elizabeth Smith, *George Smith: A Memoir with Some Pages of Autobiography*, (Private Circulation, 1902, Kindle Edition), p.87.
[124] Juliet Barker, *The Brontës*, (London: Weidenfeld & Nicolson, 1994, Kindle Edition), loc. 13200.
[125] David Cannadine, *Victorious Century*, (London: Allen Lane, 2017), p.242.
[126] *Selected Letters of Charlotte Brontë*, ed. by Margaret Smith, (Oxford: Oxford University Press, 2007), p.86.
[127] Clement K. Shorter, *Charlotte Brontë and Her Circle*, (London: Hodder and Stoughton, 1896, Kindle edition) loc 12
[128] Clement K. Shorter, *Charlotte Brontë and Her Circle*, (London: Hodder and Stoughton, 1896, Kindle Edition), loc. 5483.
[129] Charlotte Brontë to William Smith Williams, 4 October, 1847 Brontë Society BS 59
[130] Juliet Barker, *The Brontës*, (London: Weidenfeld & Nicolson, 1994, Kindle Edition)
[131] *Athenaeum*, no. 1043, 23 October 1847, p.1100.

[132] *Selected Letters of Charlotte Brontë*, ed. by Margaret Smith, (Oxford: Oxford University Press, 2007), p.88.

[133] *Selected Letters of William Makepeace Thackeray*, ed. by EF Harden, (Garland Publishing 1994) p.141. Reproduce by kind permission of the current holder of Thackeray's copyright.

[134] William Makepeace Thackeray, *Memoirs of a Victorian Gentleman*, ed. by Margaret Forster, (London: Book Club Associates,1979), p.147.

[135] *Selected Letters of William Makepeace Thackeray*, ed. by EF Harden, (Garland Publishing 1994) p.206. Reproduce by kind permission of the current holder of Thackeray's copyright.

[136] Leonard Huxley, *The House of Smith Elder*, (London: Private Circulation, 1923, Kindle edition), loc. 1112.

[137] *The Letters of Charlotte Brontë, Volume 2: 1848-1851*, ed. by Margaret Smith, (Oxford: Clarendon Press, 2000). p.301. The Henry W. and Albert A. Berg Collection of English and American Literature, The New York Public Library, Astor, Lenox and Tilden Foundations.

[138] *Selected Letters of Charlotte Brontë*, ed. by Margaret Smith, (Oxford: Oxford University Press, 2007), p.90.

[139] *Selected Letters of Charlotte Brontë*, ed. by Margaret Smith, (Oxford: Oxford University Press, 2007), p91.

[140] *Selected Letters of Charlotte Brontë*, ed. by Margaret Smith, (Oxford: Oxford University Press, 2007), p.93.

[141] *Selected Letters of Charlotte Brontë*, ed. by Margaret Smith, (Oxford: Oxford University Press, 2007), p.92.

[142] Juliet Barker, *The Brontës*, (London: Weidenfeld & Nicolson, 1994, Kindle Edition), loc. 13148.

[143] *Selected Letters of Charlotte Brontë*, ed. by Margaret Smith, (Oxford: Oxford University Press, 2007) p.94.

[144] Leonard Huxley, *The House of Smith Elder*, (London: Private Circulation, 1923, Kindle Edition), loc. 1136.

[145] Rebecca Fraser, *Charlotte Brontë*, (London: Methuen, 1988), p.280.

[146] Clement K. Shorter, *Charlotte Brontë and Her Circle*, (London: Hodder and Stoughton, 1896). p.338.
[147] *The Letters of Charlotte Brontë, Volume 2: 1848-1851*, ed. by Margaret Smith, (Oxford: Clarendon Press, 2000), p.10.
[148] Charlotte Bronte to William Smith Williams, 22 January 1848, Brontë Society, Bon 196.
[149] Eileen Fauset, *The Politics of Writing, Julia Kavanagh*, (Manchester: Manchester University Press, 2009), p.23.
[150] Karen Laird, *The Art of Adapting Victorian Literature, 1848-1920: Dramatizing Jane Eyre, David Copperfield, and The Woman in White*, (London: Routledge, 2016), p.20.
[151] *The Letters of Charlotte Brontë, Vol 2 1848-1851*, ed. by Margaret Smith, (Oxford: Clarendon Press, 2000) p.27.
[152] Margaret Smith, 'A Window on the World: Charlotte Brontë's Correspondence with Her Publishers', *Brontë Society Transactions*, xxi,, pp339-356.
[153] Clement K. Shorter, *Charlotte Brontë and Her Circle*, (London: Hodder and Stoughton, 1896, Kindle Edition), loc. 5452.
[154] *The Letters of Charlotte Brontë, Volume 2: 1848-1851*, ed. by Margaret Smith, (Oxford: Clarendon Press, 2000), p.30.
[155] Clement K. Shorter, *Charlotte Brontë and Her Circle*, (London: Hodder and Stoughton, 1896), p.372
[156] Margaret Smith, 'A Window on the World: Charlotte Brontë's Correspondence with her Publishers', *Brontë Society Transactions*, XXI (1996), p.349.
[157] Clement K. Shorter, *Charlotte Brontë and Her Circle*, (London: Hodder and Stoughton, 1896), p.374
[158] *The letters of Charlotte Brontë, Volume 2: 1848-1851*, ed. by Margaret Smith, (Oxford: Clarendon Press, 2000), p74 note 8.
[159] Margaret Smith, 'A Window on the World: Charlotte Brontë's Correspondence with her Publishers', *Brontë Society Transactions*, XXI, p.345.
[160] Charlotte Brontë to William Smith Williams, 12 May 1848, Brontë Society Gr.F3.

[161] Clement K. Shorter, *Charlotte Brontë and Her Circle*, (London: Hodder and Stoughton, 1896, Kindle Edition), loc.5611.
[162] *The Letters of Charlotte Brontë, Volume 2: 1848-1851*, ed. by Margaret Smith, (Oxford: Clarendon Press, 2000), p.74, note 7.
[163] *The Letters of Charlotte Brontë, Volume 2: 1848-1851*, ed. by Margaret Smith, (Oxford: Clarendon Press, 2000), p.74 ,note 5.
[164] *The Letters of Charlotte Brontë, Volume 2: 1848-1851*, ed. by Margaret Smith, (Oxford: Clarendon Press, 2000), p.79.
[165] Charlotte Brontë to Mary Taylor, 4 September, 1848, from a typed copy of the Brontë Letters in the Christie Library, Manchester, *Brontë Society* SB:3111.7(vi)
[166] Eric Hobsbawm, *The Age of Revolution*, (London: Weidenfeld & Nicolson, 1962, Kindle Edition), loc. 927.
[167] Helen Arnold, 'Americans and the Brontës', reproduced from *Brontë Society Transactions* in *The Brontës Then and Now*, (Haworth: The Brontë Society, 1947, 1949), p47.
[168] Elizabeth Smith, *George Smith: A Memoir with Some Pages of Autobiography*, (Private circulation, 1902, Kindle Edition), loc. 1316.
[169] Clement K. Shorter, *Charlotte Brontë and Her Circle*, (London: Hodder and Stoughton, 1896), p.385.
[170] F. Klickmann, 'Moments with Modern Musicians', *The Windsor Magazine*, 1896, p.422.
[171] Clement K. Shorter, *Charlotte Brontë and her Circle*, (London: Hodder and Stoughton, 1896, Kindle Edition), loc.5686. The Morgan Library & Museum. MA 2696.35. The Henry Houston Bonnell Bronte Collection. Bequest of Helen Safford Bonnell, 1969.
[172] Clement K. Shorter, *Charlotte Brontë and Her Circle*, (London: Hodder and Stoughton, 1896, Kindle Edition), loc. 5691.
[173] William Smith Williams, 'Royal Academy Exhibition', *John Bull Magazine*, 1 July 1848

[174] Margaret Smith, 'A Window on the World: Charlotte Brontë's Correspondence with her Publishers', *Brontë Society Transactions*, XXI, p.351.
[175] Timothy Hilton, *The Pre Raphaelites*, (London: Thames and Hudson, 1970), p.28.
[176] *The Diary of Ford Madox Brown*, ed. by Virginia Surtees, (Yale: Yale University Press, 1981) p.69.
[177] Clement King Shorter, *Charlotte Brontë and Her Circle*, (London: Hodder and Stoughton, 1896), p.387.
[178] Emily Petermann, '"These Are Not a Whit Like Nature": Lucy Snowe's Art Criticism in *Villette*', B*rontë Studies*, XXXVI (2011), pp.277-288.
[179] Jian Choe, 'Towards Modern Aesthetics: Charlotte Brontë and J. M. W.Turner', *Brontë Studies*, XLIII (2018), pp.125-135.
[180] Jian Choe, 'Towards Modern Aesthetics: Charlotte Brontë and J. M. W.Turner', *Brontë Studies*, XLIII (2018), p.126.
[181] Kirsty Stonell Walker, *Stunner*, Creativespace.com., 2011
[182] Donald Hopwell 'The Misses Brontë – Victorians', in *The Brontës then and Now*, (Haworth: The Brontë Society,1947, 1949), p.14.
[183] William Smith Williams, 'On the Importance of a Knowledge and Observance of the Principles of Art by Designers', *The Builder*, Volume 7, 24 March 1849, p.133.
[184] *The letters of Charlotte Bronte, Vol 2 1848-1851*, ed. by Margaret Smith, (Oxford: Clarendon Press, 2000) p.202.
[185] Jerry White, *London in the 19th Century*, (London: Vintage, 2008) p.50.
[186] Clement King Shorter, *Charlotte Brontë and Her Circle*, (London: Hodder and Stoughton, 1896, Kindle Edition), loc.5754.
[187] Lawrence Buell, *Emerson*, (Harvard: Harvard University Press, 2003), p.1.
[188] *The letters of Charlotte Brontë, Volume 2: 1848-1851*, ed. by Margaret Smith, (Oxford: Clarendon Press, 2000), p.135.

[189] C. Mabel Edgerley, 'Causes of Death of the Brontës', reproduced from *Brontë Society Transactions*, in *The Brontës Then and Now*, (Haworth: The Brontë Society, 1947, 1949), p.57.

[190] Diary of the late John Epps M.D. Edin embracing autobiographical records; notes on passing events; homoeopathy general medicine politics and religion etc Mrs Epps ed. Kent and Co, 279

[191] Jenny Uglow, George Eliot, (London: Virago, 1987) p.56.

[192] *The Letters of Charlotte Brontë, Volume 2: 1848-1851*, ed. by Margaret Smith, (Oxford: Clarendon Press, 2000) p.140.

[193] *The Letters of Charlotte Brontë, Volume 2: 1848-1851*, ed. by Margaret Smith, (Oxford: Clarendon Press, 2000), pp.155-7. Manuscript in private hands.

[194] Robert and Louise Barnard, *A Brontë Encyclopaedia*, (Chichester: Wiley-Blackwell, 2013), p.374.

[195] *The Letters of Charlotte Brontë, Volume 2: 1848-1851*, ed. by Margaret Smith, (Oxford: Clarendon Press, 2000, p.174.

[196] Margaret Smith, A Window on the World: Charlotte Brontë's Correspondence with her Publishers, *Brontë Society Transactions*, XXI, (1996), pp.339-356.

[197] Charlotte Brontë to William Smith Williams, 4 February 1849, Brontë Society B.S. 67.

[198] Clement King Shorter, *Charlotte Brontë and her Circle,* (London: Hodder and Stoughton, 1896), p.393.

[199] C. Mabel Edgerley, 'The Youngest Sister', reproduced from *Brontë Society Transactions*, in *The Brontës then and Now*, (Haworth: The Brontë Society, 1947, 1949), p.55.

[200] Charlotte Brontë to William Smith Williams, 25 June 1849, Brontë Society B.S. 70.

[201] *The Letters of Charlotte Brontë, Vol 2 1848-1851*, ed. by Margaret Smith, (Oxford: Clarendon Press, 2000) p.225.

[202] Charlotte Brontë to William Smith Williams, 3 July 1849, Brontë Society, B.S. 71.

[203] Clement King Shorter, *Charlotte Brontë and Her Circle,*

(London: Hodder and Stoughton, 1896), p.395.
[204] *The letters of Charlotte Brontë, Volume 2: 1848-1851*, ed. by Margaret Smith, (Oxford: Clarendon Press, 2000,) p.227, note 3.
[205] Clement King Shorter, *Charlotte Brontë and Her Circle,* (London: Hodder and Stoughton, 1896, Kindle Edition), loc.5828.
[206] Rosalie Glynn Grylls, *Queen's College 1848-1948*, (London: Routledge, 1948), p2.
[207] Margaret Mills, 'Female Education as a Theme in the Novels of Charlotte
Brontë', *Brontë Studies*, XLIII (2018), pp.71-77.
[208] Juliet Barker, *The Brontës*, (London: Weidenfeld & Nicolson, 1994, Kindle Edition), loc. 12949.
[209] The Beginnings of the Working Men's College, (London: Working Men's College), p.7.
[210] The Beginnings of the Working Men's College, (London: Working Men's College).
[211] Charlotte Brontë to William Smith Williams 24 August 1849, Brontë Society, Bon. 211.
[212] Charlotte Brontë to William Smith Williams 17 September 1849, Brontë Society, Bon. 214.
[213] *The letters of Charlotte Brontë, Volume 2: 1848-1851*, ed. by Margaret Smith, (Oxford: Clarendon Press, 2000), p.277.
[214] *Athenaeum*, no11493, November 1849, p.1107.
[215] *The letters of Charlotte Brontë, Vol 2 1848-1851*, ed. by Margaret Smith, (Oxford: Clarendon Press, 2000) p.299.
[216] Jian Choe, 'Towards Modern Aesthetics: Charlotte Brontë and J. M. W. Turner', *Brontë Studies*, XLIII (2018), p.126.
[217] *The Letters of Charlotte Brontë, Volume 2: 1848-1851*, ed. by Margaret Smith, (Oxford: Clarendon Press, 2000), p.306.
[218] Charlotte Brontë to Letitia Wheelwright, 17 December 1949, Brontë Society B.S. 72.
[219] *The Letters of Charlotte Brontë, Volume 2: 1848-1851*, ed. by Margaret Smith, (Oxford: Clarendon Press, 2000), p.312.

[220] Charlotte Brontë to William Smith Williams, 9 January 1850, Brontë Society, BS 73.
[221] Hertfordshire Mercury, June 2, 1888.
[222] *The Letters of Charlotte Brontë, Volume 2: 1848-1851*, ed. by Margaret Smith, (Oxford: Clarendon Press, 2000), p.xlviii.
[223] Gordon S. Haight, *George Eliot: A Biography*, (Oxford: Clarendon Press, 1968), p132.
[224] Jennifer Uglow, *George Eliot*, (London: Virago, 1987), p50.
[225] Rebecca Fraser, *Charlotte Brontë*, (London: Methuen, 1988), p.110.
[226] Clement King Shorter, *Charlotte Brontë and Her Circle*, (London: Hodder and Stoughton, 1896), p.399.
[227] *The letters of Charlotte Brontë, Volume 2: 1848-1851*, ed. by Margaret Smith, (Oxford: Clarendon Press, 2000), p.383.
[228] William Michael Rossetti, *Some Reminiscences*, (New York: Scribner, 1906) pp.96-97.
[229] E-mail from Cheryl Pivac.
[230] *The Letters of Charlotte Brontë, Volume 2: 1848-1851*, ed. by Margaret Smith, (Oxford: Clarendon Press, 2000) p.415. Charlotte Bronte letter to Ellen Nussey, 1850, June 12, HM 24471, The Huntington Library, San Marino, California.
[231] Charlotte Brontë to William Smith Williams, 27 August 1850, Brontë Society BS 79.6.
[232] *The Letters of Charlotte Brontë, Volume 2: 1848-1851*, ed. by Margaret Smith, (Oxford: Clarendon Press, 2000) p.287.
[233] Jane Robinson, *Hearts and Minds: The Untold Story of the Great Pilgrimage and How Women Won the Vote*, (London: Doubleday, 2018), p.22.
[234] Margaret Smith, 'George Smith, Prince of Publishers, and William Smith Williams', *Brontë Studies*, XXVI (2011), pp.75-84.
[235] *The Letters of Charlotte Brontë, Volume 2: 1848-1851*, ed. by Margaret Smith, (Oxford: Clarendon Press, 2000), p.550.
[236] Leonard Huxley, *The House of Smith Elder*, (London:

Private Circulation, 1923), p.69.
[237] *The Letters of Charlotte Brontë, Volume 2: 1848-1851*, ed. by Margaret Smith, (Oxford: Clarendon Press, 2000), p.604.
[238] *The Letters of Charlotte Brontë, Volume 2: 1848-1851*, ed. by Margaret Smith, (Oxford: Clarendon Press, 2000), p.625.
[239] Dickinson Pictures of The Great Exhibition: https://www.bl.uk/collection-items/dickinsons-comprehensive-pictures-of-the-great-exhibition-of-1851
[240] *The Letters of Charlotte Brontë, Volume 2: 1848-1851*, ed. by Margaret Smith, (Oxford: Clarendon Press, 2000), p.667.
[241] *The letters of Charlotte Brontë, Volume 2: 1848-1851*, ed. by Margaret Smith, (Oxford: Clarendon Press, 2000), p.668.
[242] Charlotte Brontë to William Smith Williams, 21 July, 1851, Brontë Society BS82.
[243] David Cannadine, *Victorious Century*, (London: Allen Lane, 2017,) p.306.
[244] Charlotte Brontë to William Smith Williams, 26 September, 1851, Brontë Society BS 83.5.
[245] Cheryl Pivac letter no 40.
[246] *The Letters of Charlotte Brontë, Volume 3: 1852-1855*, ed. by Margaret Smith (Oxford: Clarendon Press, 2004), p15.
[247] *The letters of Charlotte Brontë, Volume 3: 1852-1855*, ed. by Margaret Smith (Oxford: Clarendon Press, 2004), p.139.
[248] *The letters of Charlotte Brontë, Volume 3: 1852-1855*, ed. by Margaret Smith (Oxford: Clarendon Press, 2004), p.34.
[249] *The Letters of Charlotte Brontë, Volume 3: 1852-1855*, ed. by Margaret Smith (Oxford: Clarendon Press, 2004), p.80.
[250] Emily Petermann '"These Are Not a Whit Like Nature": Lucy Snowe's Art Criticism in Villette', *Brontë Studies*, XXXVI (2011), 277-288.
[251] *The Letters of Charlotte Brontë, Volume 3: 1852-1855*, ed. by Margaret Smith (Oxford: Clarendon Press, 2004), p.132.
[252] Charlotte Brontë to William Smith Williams, 8 April 1853, Brontë Society, Grolier F2.
[253] Clement King Shorter, *Charlotte Brontë and Her Circle,* (London: Hodder and Stoughton, 1896, Kindle Edition),

loc.5934.
[254] Clement King Shorter, *Charlotte Brontë and Her Circle*, (London: Hodder and Stoughton, 1896, Kindle Edition), loc.5940
[255] *The Letters of Charlotte Brontë, Volume 3: 1852-1855*, ed. by Margaret Smith (Oxford: Clarendon Press, 2004), p.212.
[256] *The Letters of Charlotte Brontë, Volume 3: 1852-1855*, ed. by Margaret Smith (Oxford: Clarendon Press, 2004), p.250.
[257] William Makepeace Thackeray, The *Cornhill*, volume 1, January-June 1860, pp483-498.
[258] *The Letters of Mrs Gaskell*, ed. by JAV Chapple and Arthur Pollard, (Manchester: Manchester University Press, 1966), p375. The Elizabeth Gaskell Family Collection.
[259] Elizabeth Baumer Williams in *The Macmillan Magazine*, No 382, August 1891, p279 By courtesy of the Brontë Society.
[260] *The Letters of Mrs Gaskell*, ed. by JAV Chapple and Arthur Pollard, (Manchester: Manchester University Press, 1966), 395. The Elizabeth Gaskell Family Collection.
[261] Winifred Gérin, *Elizabeth Gaskell: A Biography*, (Oxford: Clarendon Press, 1976), p161.
[262] *The Letters of Mrs Gaskell*, ed. by JAV Chapple and Arthur Pollard, (Manchester: Manchester University Press, 1966), 401. The Elizabeth Gaskell Family Collection.
[263] Juliet Barker, *The Brontës*, (London: Hachette, 1994, Kindle Edition), loc.19632.
[264] *The Letters of Mrs Gaskell*, ed. by JAV Chapple and Arthur Pollard, (Manchester: Manchester University Press, 1966), p.419. The Elizabeth Gaskell Family Collection.
[265] Leonard Huxley, *The House of Smith, Elder*, (Private Circulation, 1923, Kindle edition) loc. 1306.
[266] *The Letters of Mrs Gaskell*, ed. by JAV Chapple and Arthur Pollard, (Manchester: Manchester University Press, 1966), p641. The Elizabeth Gaskell Family Collection.
[267] E-mail from Sophia's descendent Cheryl Pivac.
[268] Jane Robinson, *Hearts and Minds: The Untold Story of the*

Great Pilgrimage and How Women Won the Vote, (London: Doubelday, 2018), p.xviii,
[269] Leonard Huxley, *The House of Smith, Elder,* (Private Circulation, 1923, Kindle Edition) loc. 1481.
[270] Jenifer Glynn, *Prince of Publishers, A Biography of the Great Victorian Publisher George Smith*, (London: Alison and Busby, 1986), p.126.
[271] Leonard Huxley, *The House of Smith,* (Private Circulation, 1923, Kindle Edition), loc. 1740.
[272] National Library of Scotland, MS23184
[273] Theodore Watts-Dunton, *Rossetti and Charles Wells: A reminiscence of Kelmscott Manor,* (1908), p.lvi.
[274] Gordon S. Haight, *George Eliot: A Biography*, (Oxford: Clarendon Press, 1968), p.379.
[275] *Selections from George Eliot's Letters*, ed. by Gordon S. Haight, (Yale: Yale University Press, 1985), 275
[276] Gordon S. Haight, *George Eliot, A Biography*, (Oxford: Clarendon Press, 1968), p.364.
[277] Hugh Witemeyer, *George Eliot and the Visual Arts*, (Yale: Yale University Press, 1979), pp.16-17
[278] J. Donald Crowley, *Nathaniel Hawthorne* (London, Routledge & Kegan Paul, 1971)
[279] *The Wedding of St George* http://www.rossettiarchive.org/docs/s150.r-1.rap.html, accessed 23 January 2018
[280] *The Letters of Mrs Gaskell*, ed. by JAV Chapple and Arthur Pollard, (Manchester: Manchester University Press, 1966), p.674-6. The Elizabeth Gaskell Family Collection.
[281] *The George Eliot Letters* Volume 4, ed. by Gordon S Haight, (Yale: Yale University Press, 1975, 1954), p.79.
[282] Leonard Huxley, *The House of Smith, Elder & Co,* (London: For private circulation, 1923, Kindle edition) loc 4000
[283] National Library of Scotland, MS23229
[284] Frederick Wicks, *Golden Lives: The Story of a Woman's Courage* (London: William Blackwood 1891)

[285] Frederick Wicks, *The Realm*, 26 April, 1895. By Courtesy of the Brontë Society.
[286] Suzanne Fagence Cooper, *To See Clearly: Why Ruskin Matters*, (Quercus, 2019, Kindle Edition), loc. 710.
[287] Andrew Hill, *Ruskinland: How John Ruskin Shapes Our World,* (London: Pallas Athene, 2019), pp242-3.
[288] *The Works of John Ruskin*, ed. by E.T. Cook and Alexander Wedderburn, (London: George Allen, 1903), XIV, p.457.
[289] Elizabeth Smith, *George Smith: A Memoir With Some Pages of Autobiography*, (Private Circulation, 1902, Kindle Edition) loc. 420.
[290] Leonard Huxley, *The House of Smith, Elder*, (Private Circulation, 1923, Kindle Edition) loc. 896.
[291] *The Works of John Ruskin*, ed. by E.T. Cook and Alexander Wedderburn, (London: George Allen, 1903), XIII, p.xx.
[292] *The Works of John Ruskin*, ed. by E.T. Cook and Alexander Wedderburn, (London: George Allen, 1903), XVII, p.xxvi.
[293] John Ruskin,*The Cornhill*, volume 1, Jan-June 1860, p543.
[294] *The Works of John Ruskin*, ed. by E.T. Cook and Alexander Wedderburn, (London: George Allen, 1903) Modern Painters, vol. v.; part ix.; chap. i.; line 7
[295] *Selections from the Writings of John Ruskin*, ed. by William Smith Williams, (London: Smith, Elder & Co, 1860), p.93.
[296] *Selections from the Writings of John Ruskin*, ed. by William Smith Williams, (London: Smith, Elder & Co, 1860), p.182.
[297] *Selections from the Writings of John Ruskin*, ed. by William Smith Williams, (London: Smith, Elder & Co, 1860), p.183.
[298] *Selections from the Writings of John Ruskin*, ed. by William Smith Williams, (London: Smith, Elder & Co, 1860), p.157.

[299] *The Works of John Ruskin*, ed. by E.T. Cook and Alexander Wedderburn, (London: George Allen, 1903), XXXVII, p.432-3. John Ruskin letter to WT Page, 22 January 1883, The Lincolnshire Archives holds the original.

[300] *Selections from the Writings of John Ruskin*, ed. by William Smith Williams, (London: Smith, Elder & Co, 1860), p.297.

[301] *The Works of John Ruskin*, ed. by E.T. Cook and Alexander Wedderburn, (London: George Allen, 1903), XVII p.li, letter to John James Ruskin from John Ruskin 9 November 1861.

[302] *The Works of John Ruskin*, ed. by E.T. Cook and Alexander Wedderburn, (London: George Allen, 1903) XVII, p.li.

[303] Clement King Shorter, *Charlotte Brontë and Her Circle*, (London: Hodder and Stoughton, 1896), p.370

[304] Andrew Ballentyne, *John Ruskin*, (London: Reaktion Books, 2015, Kindle Edition), loc. 2452.

[305] *The Works of John Ruskin*, ed. by E.T. Cook and Alexander Wedderburn, (London: George Allen, 1903) XVIII, p. xv.

[306] *The Works of John Ruskin*, ed. by E.T. Cook and Alexander Wedderburn, (London: George Allen, 1903) XXXVI, p.463.

[307] *The Works of John Ruskin*, ed. by E.T. Cook and Alexander Wedderburn, (London: George Allen, 1903), XXXVII, p.720.

[308] *The Works of John Ruskin*, ed. by E.T. Cook and Alexander Wedderburn, (London: George Allen, 1903), XXXVI, p.545.

[309] Reginald Blunt, *The Carlyle's Chelsea Home*, (London: G. Bell & Son, 1895)

[310] National Library of Scotland MS23174

[311] *The Works of John Ruskin*, ed. by E.T. Cook and Alexander Wedderburn, (London: George Allen, 1903)

XVIII, p.5.
[312] *The Journal of Education*, vol. 63, no. 16 (1576), 1906, pp. 440–440.
[313] WG Collingwood, *The Life of John Ruskin*, (London: Methuen 1893, Kindle Edition), loc. 2297.
[314] *The Works of John Ruskin*, ed. by E.T. Cook and Alexander Wedderburn, (London: George Allen, 1903), XVIII, p.lxxiii
[315] WG Collingwood, *The Life of John Ruskin*, (London: Methuen 1893, Kindle Edition), loc. 2451.
[316] WG Collingwood, *The Life of John Ruskin*, (London: Methuen 1893, Kindle Edition), loc. 2978.
[317] Elizabeth Smith, *George Smith a Memoir With Some Pages of Autobiography*, (Private Circulation, 1902, Kindle Edition), loc. 820.
[318] *The letters of Algernon Swinburne*, (London: Heinemann, 1918)
[319] With thanks to Christine Hutchison for this information.
[320] Letter from Robert Hill to Sophia Ellis 11 October 1875.
[321] E.M. Forster, *Goldsworthy Lowes Dickinson*, (London: Edward Arnold, 1934) p.4.
[322] The Autobiography of G. Lowes Dickinson, ed. by Dennis Proctor, (London: Duckworth, 1973), p.35.
[323] Edgar Jones *True and Fair: A History of Price Waterhouse*, (London: Hamish Hamilton, 1995), p.91.
[324] Philip Hamlyn Williams, *Ordnance*, (Gloucester: The History Press, 2018) p.92.
[325] EM Forster, *Goldsworthy Lowes Dickinson*, (London: Edward Arnold, 1934) p.155.
[326] Letter from Mary Robertson to Sophia Ellis 27 April 1890.
[327] Bob Meadley "A Letter to Bert" (a Medley about Chess Libraries, Dealers and Collectors) (Narromine, NSW, Australia 2001).

[328] Norman Penty, The Williams family tree.
[329] With thanks to Christine Hutchison for this information.
[330] With thanks to the Brontë Society.
[331] Robin Quinn, *The Man Who Broke the Bank at Monte Carlo*, (Gloucester: The History Press, 2016) p.29.

Printed by Amazon Italia Logistica S.r.l.
Torrazza Piemonte (TO), Italy